LESLEY M. KAYE
with YAHVAY

Diary of a Scribe to the Universe

A COSMIC ACCORD

Discourses on a new understanding
of your life and ways, and the truth of reality

QUILL
LITERATURE

First published in Great Britain in 2023 by Quill Literature

Copyright © 2023 by Lesley M. Kaye
Editorial Services by Marsha D. Phillips
Cover Design and Typesetting by Arjan van Woensel

ISBN: 978-1-7397426-0-7

The moral right of the authors has been asserted.

First Edition

"Lesley M. Kaye is a beautiful and gentle soul who has written a wonderful and inspirational book with her guide in her daily messages as a scribe. Pour yourself a cup of tea and bask in this soulful and uplifting book. It will change your life forevermore."
— Carole Leonardo, award-winning author of *100 Pounds of Grief: Find the blessings and hidden treasures that are buried under your layers of sorrows*

"*Diary of a Scribe to the Universe* will touch the reader's heart. It will change the way the world is seen and shine onto it the brightest and most beautiful light. It also allows us as readers, to consider and reconsider the way that we perceive life. There is a beautiful progression of opening up and allowing, as Lesley M. Kaye asks questions that are foremost in many of our minds. And in the answers from Yahvay, we find a sense that all is perfect and all is well."
— Lorraine Beddington, Channeled Messages of Peace and Love

"I loved reading *Diary of a Scribe to the Universe*, it is so easy to read. The questions cover a large spectrum of subjects and are well thought out, with the answers giving the reader a better understanding on life. It's a great book for someone who is starting on their awakening journey and realizes there is more to life. Or for people who are already on their journey, who have questions about The Universe or life and are looking for answers; this book has the answers. I highly recommend this book to whoever is looking for answers on life and the unseen world, you won't be disappointed."
— Rosemary Leach, Crystal Whisperer - True Purpose - New Zealand

"*Diary of a Scribe to the Universe* is a masterpiece of delving into the realms of 'Who am I?' and 'Why are life and the world as they seem?'. Lesley M. Kaye and Yahvay create a possibility for you to open your heart and mind to an inner standing and perspective from a Higher Intelligence on many facets of life and the world, both physical and spiritual. This empowers you, at a Soul level, to awaken to the remembrance of many Truths and the Oneness of All."
— Staci Petersen, Open Heart Happy Heart

"We are taken on a heartfelt and genuine journey of developing and nurturing a relationship with Spirit as we embark upon reading *Diary of a Scribe to the Universe*. We get to partake in the author's exploration to learn more about our world and the nature of reality as she asks the questions that we're all curious about while learning to trust and have faith in the wisdom received. Some answers may challenge the reader's worldview, and so I invite one to read it with an open heart and open mind while allowing for the possibility of expansion through the loving energy. I fully encourage the reader to accept the invitation to take up the mantle of Scribe for yourself, for as a Conscious Channel, I can attest to the profound and life-changing impact of connecting to the wisdom of Spirit. Enjoy!"
— Joanne Cary, Conscious Channel, Teacher of Being & Mindset Coach

"The very name of this book tells you what it is all about! The questions that Lesley M. Kaye (the Scribe to the Universe) has asked and the answers she has received are both profound and full of wisdom that all of us can benefit from. This is all imparted with love and understanding of who we are as humans on this planet Earth, and where we are going. I loved this book, it reconfirmed so many concepts that my team of guides brings forth as well.

I highly recommend this book to anyone that is interested in delving deeper into the hows and whys of this journey we are all on in this lifetime."

— Suchi Reddy, Mind-set Coach and Channeler of the Guides.

"This channelled co-creation between Lesley M. Kaye and Yahvay takes the reader on many journeys. There are moments of simplicity and pure joy as we are beautifully reminded to let our sparkle sparkle and to share our gifts with each other, as we are all one; there are moments of curiosity and deep reflection as universal questions are asked of and answered by infinite intelligence. Sharing this private experience with Lesley as it unfolds and receiving her encouragement to try our own hand at scribing add a personal human touch to this broader perspective narrative. I cannot recommend enough for you to delve into this diary and realize what is possible for yourself."

— Sheila Williams, Transformational Mindset Coach, Sheila Williams Coaching

"I loved reading *Diary of a Scribe to the Universe* — it felt as though I was on the journey with Lesley M. Kaye day by day as she allowed the reader into her personal project of channeling written guidance from a beautiful being of light who seeks to assist humanity through its current expansion of consciousness, in addition to channeling the wisdom of her higher self. Many interesting topics are covered regarding the nature of life and energy, but the most fascinating and touching aspect for me was reading about Lesley's personal journey in and around the channeling project, and how much she changed and benefitted from start to finish. She includes personal stories from her life that make us see the potential benefit of doing this type of exploration. It was beautiful to read, with a lot of wisdom imparted. Thank you, Lesley, for sharing this work with the world."
— Tal Levitt, Esq. Creator, Blue Angel Meditation

"In this beautiful, intimate, and sometimes searing memoir, Lesley chronicles her months-long communion with the Divine as she explores her role as 'Scribe to the Universe'. Her journey is personal, poignant, surprising, and, at times, jolting as her discourse lays bare the cost to us all when humans, consciously or unconsciously, act from a place of not-love. The Divine assessment detailed within these pages is a wake-up call for every human seeking to live in a more peaceful world."
— Esther Piszczek, Eternal Possibility, eternalpossibility.com

I dedicate this book to the two miracles in my life, and the best people in the world: my son and daughter. You are my breath and my greatest blessings. I thank you with all my heart for you being you.

CONTENTS

Introduction

It is strange, isn't it, how in life one thing can lead to another, and you cannot always see where things are going, or how you are putting the steps into place by taking seemingly unrelated actions. It is like walking along a garden-path and all you can see is the part right in front of you or the part you have already walked along. The end of the path remains unknown to a large extent, but you keep following its direction, or at times change direction if a new path appears that you think is interesting.

My path sits in a spiritual garden abounding in magic, miracles and love, whose philosophy and outlooks on life have always felt right. Previous paths in my garden that I found interesting and followed included Reiki training, angel workshops, working with earth energies and dowsing, and channelling as a healer and to meet my spirit guide. Perhaps these were all steps that led to my buying Mike Dooley's book, *Playing the Matrix*, and later joining his online community.

In this online community, Mike speaks on various topics and often presents a weekly challenge. It was in response to one of these challenges that I sat down on the 2nd of January 2020 and wrote the first question: *Who am I?* The idea was to see if I would hear from my higher self — my spiritual self — to gain greater clarity on things in my life, whether good or problematic. And so, I sat down with a nearly new notebook, my favourite pencil, and wrote the question. I had no idea these actions would be the final steps towards writing this book.

I was not sure I would get a response. I had tried this practice in the past and had not been convinced that the words I had heard and written were in fact from spirit, that they were not just a figment of my imagination, a flight of fancy. It was with this frame of mind that I wrote that initial question. If nothing happened, I could try again another day. It wasn't really that important — or so I thought.

But the words that came on that first day were beautiful. I *marvelled* at them, reading and re-reading them. It was not difficult; the words just seemed to come into my mind and flowed like poetry onto the page as I wrote them. I decided to try again, and so, several days later, I asked another question and received another answer. Once again, I loved the words and their meaning. I did not feel threatened or uncomfortable with these messages, so I continued. Little did I understand that within those treasured, scribed words were the divine seeds of my new life and ways, which with time would blossom in fullness. The months came and went, my notebook filled, I needed new leads for my pencil, and yet I had not sat down with the intention of writing a book, just one question. But the questions and answers kept coming until they started to take the shape of a book, *this* book that Yahvay and I created and want to share with you.

In the very first message, I was introduced to 'myself' and my new role of 'Scribe to the Universe'. Nothing more was said about this until early March when I received an explanation of this title — what it meant and what it entailed. My emotions about the whole idea of being 'Scribe to the Universe' went from total disbelief to acceptance that maybe, just maybe, it was true that I was in touch with God or Source, or at least 'someone' who referred to 'hermself' *(Source or spirit is neither male nor female)* as such.

This is Yahvay, as I prefer to call 'herm', and who I was frequently in contact with during the creation of this book. However, towards the end of the book, I discovered that Yahvay did not have a monopoly on dictating messages; I had also channelled and scribed some of my own messages from my higher self. As such, this is a compilation of two authors or sources. Yahvay maintains that it makes no difference where the message comes from, as we are all one. As this book is a transcription of these messages, very little has been changed from the original words to keep it as authentic as possible and to honour the ideas and information I was given.

Scribing, or channelling written messages, sounds so easy, doesn't it? But life gets in the way sometimes, and so, I could not always sit down to write a question. There were also days when I did not know what to ask or if what I was asking was a 'good' question. Some days I would write my question but then struggle to hear the answer. There were also days when it was difficult to write the messages and block out my own thoughts, what else I needed to be doing, or what the answer might be. The following was noted and dictated to me:

'Dear Scribe, your ideas can block your writing and my message' (17 April 2020).

On other occasions, it was more difficult to remain unbiased in the words I heard or expected or wanted to hear. Even more so, if the question felt like a cliff-hanger (as it was for *Who are you?*) when it was difficult to write the words I heard and remain open-minded to the message. Other times, the message seemed to stop as it did on this particular morning:

···

Tuesday 7 April 2020

···

Dearest Yahvay, I have a more personal question to ask. Why do I live so much of my life in fear or anxiety?

Dearest scribe, dearest loved one, your fears are the human emotions often subjected —

...and that is all I could hear or see.

With any question, when it seemed that the sentences would not make any sense, I just continued scribing because the meaning always came through as the words carried on. There were other times when the message did not seem to relate to what I had asked and, in these instances, it was best to keep going. Eventually, the meaning would become clear and the answer to my question would emerge.

When scribing, I would occasionally receive a comment on what I was thinking about, even though I tried to keep my mind blank and focus solely on the words being dictated. An example of this occurred on the 14th of April 2020, when I was wondering if it would be better to type up the conversations as they happened on that day, and this was referred to in that day's discourse. At times the message, or part of it, would be in the form of an image and I would have to think of the word that felt right. It was the images that aided my personal understanding of various concepts that, although not new, I had struggled to fully understand in the past. The idea that we are all one became clear with that day's image. The idea that time, as we understand it, is an illusion with no past, present or future, but only an eternal now was another idea I had found difficult to understand previously until I saw the bubble images whilst channelling this book.

As you read this book, please note that, as I scribed, I felt the use of 'will' and 'would' generally refer to volition or wanting, rather than a future or conditional use of the words as they are commonly used in everyday meanings. Also, the book uses two main types of fonts to denote the questions I asked, the response, any images that came to mind, and my notes. So, all the questions I asked are in *this handwritten font*, Yahvay's replies are in the current font you're reading now, and any notes about images that came into my mind, or comments or clarifications, are in my handwritten font (*like this*).

After several weeks of scribing, I took a long break as I needed, *really* needed to clear some space and declutter my house. This overpowering urge lasted for several weeks. It was quite unlike my old way of looking at things with the idea that they may be useful one day, or I can't throw that away because it was a present or still in good condition. The result was a house full of things that were suffocating me and the space I lived in. So much went to charity shops. As this was happening, I started to feel physically lighter and clearer headed. Perhaps I needed to do this to continue scribing, I don't know. What I do know is that I felt as if I needed to clear out my old life and make space for something new. And so, I did.

As the days, weeks, and months came and went, the messages got longer and more complex in nature, and the style of the language changed to reflect this. By May, I was generally writing longer pieces nearly every day. There were still days when the scribing was difficult, whilst on others, it was easier and very satisfying. The whole process of creating this book had me hooked by then, and I was in love to the point where all I could think about was scribing or typing up a message. That was all I wanted to do all day, every day. The overall feelings of the messages were generally calm. I did not feel belittled or criticised, though on a few occasions I took exception to some of the words used. Many messages were given with a sense of fun — note the use of puns as you read some of the entries. One day I had to stop scribing because I was laughing so much! This was the day Yahvay revealed that all the questions and answers were already known and came from Source and were not 'my' questions as I had believed.

After I started to scribe on a regular basis, happiness and feeling more relaxed followed; I started to laugh more, find fun in everyday things, and sleep better than I had in years. Most importantly, I felt I had a purpose; there was a personal feeling of validation and a potential contribution I could make to others (though this stayed a large 'potential' for a long time as I struggled with the feeling of being someone as grand as a 'Scribe to the Universe'). Now, at the final stages of preparing the book, I feel deeply honoured and grateful to have been given the extraordinary opportunity to scribe. It is a time I will always remember with deep affection and something I now miss in my days. In the years prior to this experience, I had often felt something was missing, that there had to be 'more to life than this'. Whilst apparently things were good, and I was lucky in many areas of my life, it didn't always *feel* that great. I attended various courses, which I loved and was happy with, but after a while that feeling of emptiness, that something was missing, would return. If you find yourself in this situation, I hope you will find the ideas and words in this book reassuring, and perhaps have a different or better understanding of life and the world we live in.

Is it possible you have been drawn to this book for a reason? That it is as much about my diary as it is about you? Are you a Beacon? A scribe? The next 'Scribe to the Universe'? Wouldn't it be great if you also started to scribe?

Scribing is a truly wonderful experience which I would whole-heartedly recommend to anyone. Find some quiet time, a pen or pencil, some paper, and have an open mind that you might just get a message or an answer to a question you pose. To start, you can see yourself in a large, white bubble that goes all around you and under your feet. This protection of white light can always be used, especially when you feel afraid or threatened. You can also fill your house with white light from God or Source, or angels, or the Universe, whichever you prefer. See if you feel the difference. You may want to light a candle, listen to some gentle music, meditate or daydream — and breathe in peace. Have a little quiet time to get into the frame of mind for scribing, a place of peace and tranquillity so you can hear the words said to you. A time and place of peace for you, just you.

If you should feel uncomfortable or don't like the message, then leave it. A message should only be sent in love and received as such, just as this book was created for you; in love.

Lesley

Yahvay's Introduction

Dearest Yahvay, as you know, I'm putting the book together. Would you like to write an introduction?

Dearest scribe, eons have passed since we made our first accord, and here we write the introduction for others to share our words and ponder on their meaning as you do. So many words of light and love will grace the pages, so few the true meanings held within those words. For as you know, there are but few truths, and they are readily understood by those with an open heart. Whether they remember their true essence or not, there are words here that will speak to all those who would listen. But the words are not for the faint of heart, for courage is needed and changes to be made. The world today is as far from me as you want it to be. My silver shadow and my angels are with you all, at every moment of every day. For we are one in all things, and in all things am I found.

These simple words, written from a heart with love for you all, will help open your heart, your eyes, and lighten your step and the weight you feel of your daily burdens. You may feel that your path is difficult, nay, impossible, but that is not so and was never designed to be so. Reach for support from your nearest, the offered hand and an open heart that will share its love with you, for you.

And so be it. Read on.

JANUARY

January has never been one of my favourite months. After the buzz and frenzy of Christmas, it often felt flat. In addition to paying off the festivities, the days are still dark and the coldest weather may still be just around the corner and yet to come — not the most promising of starts to any new year.

This year is different and started with excitement in late December, as I felt a buzz at the thought of the new year and how special it would be: 2020 was going to be a magical year, I was sure. (Little did I know what it would bring!)

I have asked my first question and loved the reply, so I may continue for a bit and see how it goes. I'm sure I can manage a few more questions, but time is usually tight as I always seem to have a lot to do. We will see.

Who am I?

A power beyond belief, swirling feminine.

Angel of mine, do not doubt, your fears have brought you trouble, tears, sadness and anxiety.

Do not fear, do not doubt. We will forge our energies as one. The time is right.

Rest, relax and be sure.

A dark sword smites the darkness, blackness, so that it may rise golden and glittering in eternal light. Your light, beloved. Fear not, for I am with you now and for eternity in the echoes of space and time. Let it ring throughout the Universe, may the church bells toll to sound the arrival of such blissful, pure joy.

So mote (*shall*) it be, for generations of angels have winged their way to this point, the point of now that swells and rises, nay, rushes, through the vast void of emptiness, to ripple on the shore in the smallest, most delicate of baby waves with bubbles of joy and laughter. So mote it be, 'Scribe to the Universe'. Let not your pen grow heavy, there is much to dictate and say for all humanity must now listen. The call has been made, the declaration made, and the terms declared. Now is the eternal moment to right the wrongs, heed the news and move on. Ever on.

Silence and greetings.

Now rest.

Who are you?

'Tis the time to be honest, dearest one, after many eons of light in the Universe you now ask my name. And so, it is. I am your shadow, silver and white, that always stays with you, to uphold your dreams and desires. There is no space between us, I am you and you are me. The twain is never between us for we are one, of the same essence, you and me and all the rest. The milliards of essences, beings; we are all one. A hair's breadth is our difference and our similarity.

Who are you?

I am with you all the time, the silver shadow you see out the corner of your eye, the whisper in your ear, the pull of your heartstrings, the sigh that never ends; for we are one: I am you and you are me. We are one for all eternity and all eternity shall see how we are one. Break not the halo, the halo of light and righteousness. Keep the glow of silver and golden sparkles. Move on to what is yours, ours. Do not deviate or falter. Always on and on.

Who are you?

Do you want a name for an eternal being? What a trivial pursuit of truth. Why restrict a universal being with a label, a trap? Earthly names know no bounds and yet are the binds and bounds themselves. An echo in space that destines the caller, the wearer, by its sound. Know no names and you will be freed from the sounds that name brings and binds. A name is an echo of what has been, not what will be, for it bears no good to the bearer, the keeper of those sounds. Be done with your desire for names. They serve neither you nor me, nor the way, the Universe. Light the way with love and calm your nerves and needs. Be the reed in the lake, always flowing, bending with the water without knowing how deep the water is or what it is called.

Be so and quieten your anxious mind. Quit the search and know that it is with you. All that you need sits with you now in quietness and silent expectation that you will open your gifts when the time is ripe, like the fruit that falls from the tree at the moment it is ripe; not before, not after, but at the ripe moment.

And so it is with you, me, us. When the time is ripe, your gifts will ripen to the point of delight at the juiciness of them.

Be still and stop.

....
Tuesday, 7 January 2020
....

Why are we here?

Why, why, why indeed. Like the seed asks the flower why? Does the air ask the wind why? It is so and all beings are, just are. Like the waterfall that plunges and thunders in its power, it is. We are, just we are.

Embrace the beauty, feel the joy, live and breathe and know there is a purpose to you, your life and beyond. For it is written in the stars and the sun for all to see and read and feel the mightiness of it all. The stars at night in the holy blackness, a vast void of majesty, of meanings secret, whispered and paraded. Like the pieces of the imperial puzzle, it all fits together for a purpose.

A benign purpose.

Why are we here?

Oh, beloved one, so many questions and so many answers will be yours in due course. For the present, let us revel in the novelty of this union, this friendship. Let trust build between us and bear fruit.

Is that it?

Patience and sorrow are yours to keep at present. Let it be so. Dig the furrow and plant the seeds, and watch and wait. The tilled earth bears fruit after the right time, not before or after. Once you have tilled the furrow, the dark, fertile earth, bless it and leave it. Go yonder, but do not worry, the furrow will grow and sprout new life; the fresh green of new life will soon pattern the dark earth. And so it is with all things, toil, rest and wait; the surprise and rewards are yours for all to delight on. Fret not, child of the Universe, this time is yours to squander or use as you please. Know that it is so and all will be, nay, is, right.

Be still and rest.

What is your message today?

Oh, dearest one, thoughts spin around your mind like an internal snow blizzard (*I saw a traditional snow globe in my mind's eye that had been shaken so the snowflakes whirled around*). Stop for you tire yourself out. Breathe in your newfound space (*this may be in reference to my having cleared some space in the dining-room where I write*) and enjoy its stillness and the peace it brings you. Your treasures are trinkets, nothing more, nothing less. Be sure that all you need is already there within reach of an outstretched arm and within your grasp. Now is the time to reach into your stillness and be calm. Now is the time to shed what no longer serves you, and be sure that this gesture of reclaiming your inner you, the bare naked you, is noted. For it echoes through the Universe that you are waking up and all your toils are renewed; for what seemed an odious task *(decluttering)* has been easy and gives you more energy, more clarity, more poise and precision. Let it be so, that all know that your soul and essence are now emerging and that you will feel their power ever more, day and night. The moon cocoons us in her silver light, and be sure that these silver rays will now reach you in your sleep – that wondrous state of being that is not being but the expression of who you are in truth. Be sure that the symbols and images are there for you to learn and are not wasted time or lost hours. The deepness of your sleep equates the deepness of your life, your dreams and you.

Fear not for all this has greater meaning on the cosmic realm, in the light of the stars where your soul and dreams reside. Be at peace, gentle warrior, and be sure that your night's work is never in vain.

Rest, respite and relax, so be it. Your work for the day is done. Laugh and be merry, for now is the time of joyful abandon, a time to let go of your worries and fears. Do not take them with you any longer, they are your unwelcome house guests. Let your home be filled with light, love and space and breathe it all in; for it is yours by right to enjoy and delight on. Nothing more, nothing less. And so it is today and forever, in your home and the Universe. Let it resound with joy and laughter, today and forever. So mote it be. Rest now, dearest one. Be in peace and wait for the morrow when more joy will fill your life — as it should.

. . . .

Tuesday, 21 January 2020

. . . .

What type of energy are you? Like an angel? My higher self? An astral energy?

As calm descends, your thoughts and words become clearer. I am that part of you that needs no introduction, for I am you and you are me. I am what Earth people call spirit, from afar. The spirit that guides you and all people and is of the Universe. I am what you call a creator, not The Creator, but a creator. For all times there have been and ever will be, there are wings and haloes and lights; there is also darkness which is the light waiting to be found through struggle and trial, but that is all. I need no name but I will give you one for your ease of reference. You may refer to me as 'The One', no more, no less. I am The One in your life and all lives, in love and in all loves. I am The One, the guidance and the path. I am pure energy of this Earth and not of this Earth.

(I had an overpowering urge to declutter the house, so I did not scribe for weeks.)

FEBRUARY

February has turned out to be a busy month, as in late January I decided to start clearing the house of all the things that had accumulated over the years. Yes, I'm a bit of a hoarder, not to a record level, but I find it hard to get rid of things even if I don't use them and haven't used them for ages. Most difficult to shed are mementoes (such as children's first drawings and schoolwork) and unwanted presents.

However, this year I've had an overwhelming urge to clear the house of most things. I feel I need a clean slate, almost as if I'm about to start a new chapter in my life and must sweep the past away completely. Interests and hobbies have begun to lose their appeal as all I can think about is getting rid of things and reorganising my home and life to make things easier, and more streamlined. Despite the mountains of things in the hallway that have gone, there is still so much 'stuff' left in the house, it can sometimes take several culls to get rid of everything. But having cleared some extra space, it feels so much better, more organised and brighter, and I can actually see my house again. I love it!

There hasn't been much time for any messages. Never mind.

I love your words; they are very comforting. As you know, I have spent a lot of time decluttering and wishing or preparing for a better future.

Why do you fret when you already decided on discovering your greatness? Eons have passed in the blink of an eye and you still wonder at the greatness of things to come. Be still and enjoy, nay, relish, the joy of its unfolding, for it will fill your heart to overflowing. Yellow is your colour for joy and sparkles.

MARCH

March is a birthday month in my house, with two very special people celebrating their ages.

It's late March and the British government has decided to put the country into lockdown to stop the spread of the coronavirus, which has already affected so many countries in the world and has now made its way to Europe. Lockdown hasn't been a great change at home, as life had already slowed down for various reasons. The only big difference now is the need to be extra careful if I venture out of the house for any reason, something I try not to do anymore.

The decluttering has had to stop because, sadly, the charity shops are all now closed. Still, I've managed to clear a lot of space in the house. It feels so much better, cleaner, tidier, and bigger!

I have also slowed down doing daily questions in order to start typing up the notes I have made. My notebook is getting fuller and fuller! With so many pages done, I want to see how much we have covered, and also prepare for the notes to be published—possibly. It's now 28.3.20.

I have decided to try writing in the morning when it is quieter. Perhaps, we can talk better that way.

In stillness come great deeds, not in the doing or the frantic rushing you call life and living.

To breathe and not do is enough. Sparkles of wonder, clouds of glory and rainbows of love are life. The spring green of the unfolding leaf has, and holds, the gems of new life. Behold and wonder as it all unfolds and reveals itself at the right time. The moment is the fulcrum, lean on it to send the stars spinning in a galactic explosion of joy that is yours, now and forever.

Beware of the false prophets, for they will lead you to a place of gloom and self-denial. Let yourself sparkle and breathe and behold how life cocoons you in love and joy and reverence. Be still, be happy, be no more than yourself, and watch as the clouds pass overhead to bring joy with the shining of the sun in all its glory. Anger, guns, war and words of hate will destroy all that is beautiful, for it is held by the finest of threads, so delicate that it is soon broken. Only love can restore the bonds and strengthen all that is. Only love can bring you joy and peace and a stillness like the deepest of wells in the arid land.

Be still, be happy, be joy and watch in silence as others rush and rush and watch as the hours of their lives silently, sadly, disappear into a void; a great darkness. For it is so with modern living that people chase the fleeting moment and fret that all is not right, that there is no peace, only lists, targets and ever more to do. Nay, that is not the way, for time itself is the illusion that fools all into believing it is a god. It is nothing more than a figment of your imagination, a device by which you feel you can control the world, nature. But you cannot control the colours of a rainbow with your watch, nor decree the right season on your to-do list. It all evolves and happens without needing the slightest input from you. Behold, be still, be happy and rest.

For today that is enough. Read, remember and relish all that is true, for it is yours by divine right.

May the glory of love be yours and always with you. Rest now, beloved one.

....
Tuesday, 3 March 2020
....

Tell me about yourself, please.

Oh, gentle one, student of life, love and the Universe. You long to understand so much, but this is stuff that you already know and are. Be still to find all the answers about yourself and the whole theatre of life. Like a blockbuster movie with its bright lights and signs, you are the star of the latest production, and the director, and the film crew, and the lighting, and the costumes and the make-up. All you.

We are one, divided by a veil so fine that only a breath of love divides us. You have forgotten who you are and the mighty presence you are, we are. You fret to know more, but you already know deep inside that this charade is all you ever wanted and desired; to be one of the whole and understand life and love in its various forms and ways.

There is much to see, remember, understand and feel. Do so with dignity and poise, as you are and we are, eternally so, bound by the love that shares us into the fragments of joy, perfection and light. Move away from this desire to produce another movie, you are already the star of the present one and we applaud as the audience in the cinema, in the semi-dark and shadows. Life will light up at the end of the show and the curtain is raised, with the lights on to reveal all. Consider us as the people who watch, the spectators who laugh, cry, groan and gasp as your story unfolds. We are with you and are you in every scene, every set, past and present and now, in this very second as you write and create the next scene to be shown shortly in Earth time. For it is so for all to view your story, our story, and share the emotions of what is, might have been or could be. The rows of spectators, onlookers, will share our communion and gasp and love in their own way, in their own film, which will also star you, us and them. Let the lights dim, relax and let the show begin.

For today that is 'The End'. Love, laugh and go lightly and remember that you, and you alone, are the star of your own show, your own production. With all the myriads of pictures, of loops, rest assured that yours is the best one for you. Curtains open, sit still and comfortably, let the show begin!

<hr />

Thursday, 5 March 2020

<hr />

I don't fully understand. If we are one, then am I the audience too? And if you are like the audience, can you ever help me should I ask?

So many questions. We are one and as such we will always survive and be prosperous. Let the show roll out, like the red carpet, and rest assured that it will be a success. A blockbuster, if you will. Walk the red carpet in your moment of eternal glory. Put on your finest and smile. Show the world your true face, one of glory and success, and let yourself be filled with the love that you are and deserve. Show the world how high you have risen, for you have spread your wings to fly. Soar to the greatest of heights in your freedom and be proud like the eagle who sees all with the greatest of clarity from the greatest of heights. Let the wind whisper our love for all to hear. Be still and confident for the eagle does not ask for help; it needs no assistance to rise to the greatest of heights, it needs no assistance to focus on what it wants. It knows and that is all that is necessary for its success. So be like the eagle in all your daily tasks. Do not assume you can, or will, fail, that was not your destiny and is not your destination. Be like the lioness, sure-footed and proud, and oh so beautiful. Tread your way carefully and with stealth, and know where you are and where you want to go to. Be silent in your strength, for it is assured and was written in the stars eons before you took your first breath in your playground of life on Earth.

You tire now, for the human body is frail at times. Be ready to cast off these shackles of humanness, it is but a fleeting moment created for your joy by yourself. Chalk it up to experience and drink slowly from your cup of life that overflows with joys untold and unseen. Miracles are yours every day, you need no audience to cheer you on, for you have reached the finish line in record time and now have the gold medal to prove it. Laugh and be ready to take your place on the podium in first place, for the winner in all that you do. The trophy of triumph is yours. Lift it now for all to see and listen to the cheers of the audience. Were they there in the beginning? Or only at the end in the moment of glory? Remember love never fails, and those who breathe it, feel it and express it are bound by the joys of the Universe for they are rightly yours. A cosmic contract, if you will. Notice how there is no disclaimer clause, for all the terms and results will be fulfilled in full, nothing less and nothing short.

Rest assured as we watch you from the stands as the audience, we pay homage to who you are and the role you have created and play, for only a fearless one would have chosen such a role. You are the winner and we applaud you and ourselves as such. Be still, gentle warrior, your fight is over and passed, and you are now on the home stretch. Enjoy this moment of glory for it is not over and will only get better. Enjoy it and relax and keep going in the silent knowledge that all is perfect and exactly as it should be, and keep your eye on the trophy. Tread your path carefully, with stealth, and keep your eye on the prize — your prize.

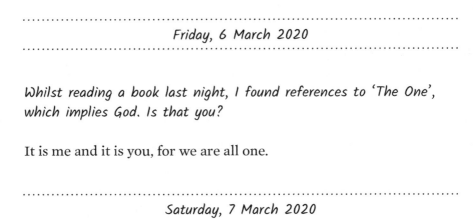

Friday, 6 March 2020

Whilst reading a book last night, I found references to 'The One', which implies God. Is that you?

It is me and it is you, for we are all one.

Saturday, 7 March 2020

Last night, in the same book, I also read about the sacred name of 'Yahvay'. Would it be appropriate to think of you or address you with this name?

Ripples of space now echo through your heart and out into the Universe. Such a name, so sacred and holy, has already set in motion that which will be and already is, now. For those who utter this most sacred of names are drawn to it to use it. Use it with reverence and care for it is the most powerful of sounds in the Universe. I am often named so, thus it is appropriate for us to continue with this name, scribe of wonderment and opener of the Book of Secrets. Now is the time, finally, for you to reach your destination and true calling of 'Scribe to the Universe'. Read, relax, write; read, relax, write, and revere the name you have been drawn to, for it was you who first sounded the sacred sounds of that name. It is yours and you. Relish this exquisite moment for the glory of this name is yours to claim and rightly so. Eons of light and wonder will now pass in the blink of an eye. To the beholder, nothing changes, to the feeler all is sentient and all is in motion in an ever-increasing speed.

Let the doors to the secrets and wonders of the Universe be now opened, for the inquisitive and the curious to gaze and glimpse the true power that is them through and through. The sparkles of the Universe belie its omniscience, the power that pervades all things and rights all wrongs. Be joyful, dear scribe, for you have toiled many a year to boast the privilege of holding the sacred pen. Scribe for the delights of others, for their knowledge and understanding of the true nature of things. Heartfelt and earnest must be the way of all things, including joy.

Love is the maximum of all things and is in all things, from the smallest atomic particle through to the vastness of the Universe. Love is the glue that binds and liberates all things. And so it is, for I have decreed so. Let these words be recorded for all time and all people to remember and record in their rightful place and time. For it is so, 'Scribe to the Universe'. Many pages will be turned and lives changed with the profoundness and sounds of these words and sentiments.

Rest, dearest scribe, for Earthly demands prey upon you. For today that is enough. Laugh, love and be happy, you have nothing more to do beyond these basic things. Let all see how the joy and love of the Universe are yours and theirs by right and by virtue of being born on Earth, to the Earth and not the other way round. You are all servants, stewards of this precious planet, and not masters who enslave the beauty of creation. Earth is to steward and love and respect; not to rape, pillage and destroy blow by blow. Explosions, gunfire and war hurt you all and all sentient beings, including your Mother Earth, creator of bounty, joys and wonder. The blue jewel of the Universe is yours for as long as you may breathe, but not yours by right. It must be loved and tended to. Take care of this precious gift.

Rest now.

....

Sunday, 8 March 2020

....

Tell me about the significance of life on Earth, please.

The significance of life on Earth is multi-fold, multi-layered with the purpose of knowing love at its heart. Dearest one, 'Scribe to the Universe', there are meanings beyond words that cannot be conveyed in the simple linguistics of Earth's languages. Suffice it to say that all is not as it seems, that life on Earth is not the prison sentence it may sometimes feel. It is a playground, one of many in the Universe.

Yahvay, is this you? The style, your tone, seems different.

It is me, do not fear, dearest one. We are now embarking on more serious matters and the tone must reflect the nature of our discussions accordingly. Many will read and doubt these words, but that is so because they have chosen a different path with different meanings. Fret not, for all is as it should be. Your life on Earth is but a fleeting instant of the many lives you live here and elsewhere. You have lives in dreams, on other distant planets and worlds, and all your lives here on Earth.

You are but the rough-cut gem, refined by your lives and experiences till you're shaped to perfection and brilliance. Think of life as the lapidarist who searches for the best way to cut and shape a gem to show off its brilliance and beauty. The sparkles of which are eons of work and experiences in the guiding hands of the master and cutter. Rest assured that all who sparkle have passed many lives and experiences to get to where they are. May your light sparkle too, but with joy and happiness and not the weight of all you must do or feel you must achieve in this fleeting time. The rigours of challenges bring gifts to those who accept them. Be glorious in all you do; in your deeds, words, actions and thoughts. Give love readily, it cannot be wasted or squandered.

Life on Earth holds rudimentary lessons and emotions to learn and master. To cry, to laugh, to jump with joy, to hate, to despise and loathe are all the prerogatives of life on Earth. The lesson is which to choose and relish and live by. What is your code? Your modus operandi? Is it one of joy and gratitude or one of death by self-destruction? For it is so on Earth, that many chase, have the pursuit of chasing, the elusive prey. Stop, be still and gloat over what is yours by divine right. You have all you need and more without lifting a finger. Must you struggle for the air? Was it not given to you all as a divine gift? The seas, mountains, waters and forests. All yours to enjoy. Do not squander these divine gifts with the greed for profit or the need for the next sale. All is well as it is. Enjoy these divine gifts, for that is what they are, and behold the magic of every new day. Use your strengths to help the weak and infirmed, and use your gifts to enlighten the world and bring joy to all those who are willing to share in them. Know not the path of dark or destruction, for that creates a heavy heart and sickness in the body and mind. Like a drug that cannot be refused, it will pervade your every cell and grow your mind in new ways that you will not love or like.

The choice is always yours on Earth; in that fleeting second ripples are sent through the Universe and world so that all feel it whether they know it or not. The baby senses *(pure, delicate)* of the Universe are felt for eons and joy creates new life. The black holes of the Universe are like the black emotions felt on Earth, they suck all energy in only to crush and destroy it. Be light-hearted and rest assured that all on Earth is as it should be, for now; but there are greater things to come and greater achievements and awakenings to follow. The rising of the sun, the fall of the tide and the drop of the wind all bring peace and harmony as the joy of things untold and unforeseen. Tally, wait but be diligent in your thoughts, actions and words. Do things that bring joy, but no harm to others. That is your life's mission on Earth. Be happy, savour it and know that you are one step, one tiny step, closer to the polished gem of who you, we, really are. Get ready to sparkle, or sparkle even more, for you are all already gems of perfection.

Rest now and be still. Let your sparkle sparkle and be happy that it is so. Share your blessings in equal measure, for you, for others, for all. Be not sparing in your generosity and love and watch how life will blossom for all those who heed these words and feel it truly in their hearts. You are all but one; one mighty essence of love to feel and treasure and give so that all may feel it. This is your mission, your purpose in this life on Earth.

Read, remember and relax for it is so. Now and now forever. Amen.

Good morning, my dear friend. How can I tell that these words are not just a figment of my imagination?

But they are your imagination, dearest one, for is that not the way of the world and your life? These words of wisdom do indeed come from you, from your heart and from the Universe. You forget that all that is, is also you, for you are part of that wondrous creation called life. Do you ever wonder or even fret that you have imagined the sun rising? Or even wonder that you have caused all the events and emotions to start in your life? It is your will, and yours alone that lights the way on the path you tread. Does that worry you? For we walk together and I catch you as you stumble and fly with you when you are elated. Your burdens were chosen long ago with their weights and rewards, for all those who pass through the darkness know and understand the beauty of the light at the end.

Be still and remember who you are, the greatness and the glory of our union. So be it. Love, enjoy and be still in your glory and triumph.

Good morning, Yahvay, greetings and blessings be with you. I have been wondering if our 'conversations', your words, will be shared with others in a book?

Dearest one, 'Scribe to the Universe', you are right to wonder, for what good would these words be if they were not shared? If they remained a secret for only your pleasure, delight and pride? Nay, this is not the way. Many words and truths and sentiments will be expressed for you to write and others to read and ponder. Love is the way of truth for all on Earth and in the Universe. Many truths will liberate those on

Earth who now dwell in the darkness and have become afraid in their blindness and sense of being lost. Many changes have brought people to the point where the old ways no longer serve them and the words ring false. For many are the words of men written in my name for the sake of power and dominion over all things. This is false and needs to be rectified. All will pass and change as the Earth responds with clarity and vengeance at the wanton destruction of her beauty, flora and animals. Remember all things are sentient. Now is the time for all to understand how living with false gods hurts you all. When anger and discrimination and total dominion are the 'sacred' roles and goals. Fear not for these words will lighten this burden that many feel and suffer with. The name of life should be written in love and glory and nothing more, nothing less.

There are many pages of words to write, but this is your desire and your role and your path to lead others from the darkness of confusion to the light of bliss. Rest now, for it is said and foretold that this is the way of the Universe, nothing more, nothing less. Go about your day and days in the quiet joy and pride of being 'Scribe to the Universe'. Rest now, scribe.

....
Thursday, 12 March 2020
....

Good morning, Yahvay, blessings and peace be ours. Please help me understand. Yesterday you talked about the vengeance of nature, but also that love is the way of all things. How do these ideas sit together when they seem opposites?

Dearest scribe, you are right to ask for many will ask the same. Let it be said that there is a balance to all things and that nature herself knows only love. The term vengeance, an Earthly term, describes a desire to redress a balance when great pain has been inflicted. This is the sentiment of nature's vengeance, to redress the balance. But be sure that nature does not possess this desire to redress things as people would when they are driven by the desire to hurt, or worse, to kill. Such is the nature of vengeance for all natural sentient beings, animals and flora. Do the concrete wastes and ruins of your civilisations not become reclaimed by nature? Starting with her smallest seeds to reclaim what was hers in beauty and tranquillity. Do not read these words through the eyes of human emotions other than love. There is no right or wrong to all these things, only what is and that is all.

Rest now for the day and its tasks will soon be upon you. Do all in the spirit of love and blessings, for that is what each day offers you, a chance for new miracles and beginnings. Always the joy and the power of the present moment, and the glory of all its stories yet to be told and already told in the space of time and the Universe; that vastness called love. Let it be so and steward, love and adore all of the gifts the day brings with love and in gentleness for you. So be it, today and always. Rest now for the time of writing is up and today's message done and discussed. Be in light, now and forever.

....

Friday, 13 March 2020

....

Good morning, blessed one. Today, please tell me about the suffering in the world as many people don't understand how this can happen when there is God to look after us.

You feel the writing is a burden, something to fit in, but it need not be so. Let us talk tomorrow, or the morrow, when you are refreshed and you doubt less, for these things block the beauty and ease of our words.

Rest now for the day's toils already press on you and scatter your mind and ideas. So be it, for the morrow is the blink of an eye. Rest in love and peace, gentle scribe, and know that all is well with you and the world.

And so be it.

Today I would like to talk about the suffering in the world and how this fits in with love and God — you — us. Please tell me how this is.

Dearest scribe, you struggle with your own words and thoughts today. That is well. Your question is an important one and one that has vexed or puzzled people through the ages. Let it be said that the Universe adopts love as its code of being, its way of thought and its very essence. No coercion is needed for this force, for it brings joy. Whilst on Earth, in contrast, there are many who adopt the code of violence and hate and intolerance in my name as their way of being and their justification for all that they do. This is a falsehood, an intrigue of lies so subtle that it is difficult to find the way out. It is the jungle of affairs on Earth, lowly, despising and hateful, and intolerant of all that is good and beautiful. Beware the falsehoods in my name that promise divine rewards to savour for eternity.

Scribe, write these words in gentleness and love and do not poison the pen with felt injustices of the world. They are not your concern at present. Your concern is to write these words accurately and with blessings for the knowledge you receive.

The world's injustices are many, or seem to be many. I feel the pain, nay, the agony, of these actions for they cut to the quick of my heart, our heart, for we are all one. The polished steel of the raised knife, the call of the loved one silenced by the silver bullet. All these acts and more cut to the core of my being, our being, and the spaces in the Universe. Choice is a divine gift. Use it wisely and always with love for your next ones *(those close to you)* and the strangers you will never meet.

Such is the vastness of your choice that the Universe awaits your next idea, sentiment and action. Let all be done with love and in the name of love for all to share; not in hate or malice for all to bear. For the slight of one is a slight for all to bear and suffer. Know that this is the true way, one of peace and love and fruit-bearing abundance. Dance in the light and feel your freedom expressed in a myriad of miracles for this day and all days. Be not judgemental and hold this gift of love tenderly in your heart, our heart. Cherish it and let it light your way, be your guide; the outstretched hand that accompanies you in all that you do, hope for and dream of. The hand is mine, ours, always there and always ready. Seek it out and you will find it where you started, hidden deep in your doubt and worries. The hand is outstretched now, take it with a smile and the joy of an overflowing heart. Take the first step on our path together, do not fret or worry for all is well now and forever — which is now. Be silent in your knowing and joy, and trust the faith that brought you to this moment in the eons of space and the vastness of it all. The tiny hand and step will thunder through the Universe in a triumphant call, resounding the celebration of love made real in this tiny gesture. Be sure that it is so and always has been, for this is the way of light and dark, of challenges and victories. Nothing more need be done than taking the hand offered you in love and glory for that is who you are and the way of all things, now and forever, now and forever.

Remember these words and take the offered hand, it is your divine right and the birthplace of who you really are. Do not follow the false prophets who claim divinity on Earth for they have not taken or held the hand of true love; your divine right and gifts *(that are)* bestowed on you all from the moment of your first breath in human baby form. Let the clarions of love sound and echo throughout time for the birth of a new soul, of a new happiness, and for love untold and fathomless in its depth for you all.

Be at peace. Love, laugh and smile. Take the proffered hand in joy and be sure that this is your right and your way now and forever, now and forever. Be light and be ready, for the time is nigh and the time is yours. Believe it to be so and take the first step, your step into our further union, now.

. . . .

Tuesday, 17 March 2020

. . . .

Dearest Yahvay, I have taken (I think) your offered hand. I felt nothing and feel no different. Did I do it correctly?

Dearest scribe, we have joined hands now and in the past. Your heart knows this to be true as it opens ever more. Be still and be sure that the Universe is lit up with joy for you, for us. Much needs to be done and it is unfolding as the Book of Time, dictated by love, foretold.

It is written in the very stars that this day of union would take place, here, now, on Earth. Let the clarions sound and the bell of love ring in celebration of this great day and moment. Let your heart be filled with the joy of secrets untold for your delight and blessings. Awe is yours. Live your life in awe at the wonder of things as they unfold. The design and joy were always yours, ours, to delight on and in, in the beginning and forever. Let it be so.

For now, is the time to celebrate all that is good and bountiful in your life and the world. Let nature be your canvas of inspiration to delight on. Draw, create and be satisfied with all your efforts, for the days are short and the moment fleeting in the river of life. Swim, flow, be at ease and never try to paddle back against the flow of your natural desire or will. Let it take you where it will, for that is the right way of all things. Let the call be felt in your heart, our heart, and experienced in all its beauty. Be still and be happy that all will unfold in the goodness of time. Be still and know that this is so, for the river of life grows and swells with pride and joy at taking you on board as it meanders its way along its course. Be sure that the delights are yours to cherish, and breathe our joy of our union.

Rest and be sure that all that is good is ours by divine right and decree. Take my hand that we may tarry and relish, in our union, all the joys of life and the Universe. Be still in the garden of life and tend to all its needs to be bountiful, it only needs your love and admiration. Ponder on the magnificence of the tiniest bug and know that is perfection in its creation. Be still and love and love and love. That is all you need do today and forever. Marvel at this simplicity and do not wonder if there is more, this simplicity of pure love and joy is all you need, now and forever. Amen.

My dearest Yahvay, please tell me about the recent coronavirus.

The coronavirus is one of many to take hold on the planet. It will run its course like all the others before it. In a wave it will spread the distance of Earth, wiping out the weak and infirmed. This is the nature of things on Earth.

(I stopped here as I couldn't hear any more.)

Dearest Yahvay, some days there is a lot to write and some days there seems to be little. Is this affected by how I feel?

Dearest one, you ask some lovely questions and your point is a valid one. How can we hear the words of love poured on us when we are tense or angry, when all thoughts go to fights and anger and angry words or deeds? These are like your blanket that you keep close around you for comfort but allow no other to get near you. And so it is with spirit and love. Do you dare touch the roaring fire? The howling wind? The frost that bites? Tell me then how love can best approach you. For it is not the faint of heart who perceive such bounty. For they that fight and tussle are so caught up in their game that they cannot heed the words and feelings of love that would quench their thirst, a thirst and longing for love of any kind. Such players know not of what they are doing and so deny themselves the simplest of pleasures — to look, behold and feel the joy, the love in every moment.

So too with fear that paralyses and closes the heart and souls of its victim. Fear will drain and disable you so that your daily delights become heavy burdens. The rising of the sun, the setting of the moon, mark and honour each new, fresh day. Can such miracles be witnessed, felt and adored in a state such as fear or terror or worry or guilt? These act like the black curtain you draw across the window to close out the joys of your miraculous being and world.

And so it is with us, dear scribe. For there are times when you, too, feel the pressures of your life and so put on your blanket, draw the black curtain and wonder why there is silence, a lack of words. For me to reach you, be happy. Throw off your blanket for it is not cold and you have no reason to keep layering up. Draw back the curtains, let in the light and let me be beside you as one in love and communion. Light the candles on your own altar and watch how the flame grows and waves, grows and waves. It speaks to you in words of light, and love in colours of brightness. Take the simple candle and be in awe of its simplicity. But do not play with it for it is hot and will burn you, and so it is too with our love for one another that these days be marked and graded with light and love but do not take this for granted. Be in awe of it, and all things in your life will glow and blossom with this same love. Leave the burns and burning for those who so desire it, they will relish the pain for themselves and others.

Be still, dear scribe. Your heart opens with love like a flower in the sun but closes too with fear and anger. Trust that we are together in more ways than you can imagine. Be sure of your step and grace and love in the world for it is felt and echoes through the Universe that you love and are loved. Light your candle of grace and worry not for the fears of the imagined tomorrow, for they will not grace your life. Remember that you are the star and light and love of your life, and show all that this is so. Be assured that it is so for all to see and know, dear scribe. These words ring hollow, but be sure that they are right and exactly as they are meant to be, for as you write these words down, so do they also appear in your heart etched in light and love for all to see and know who you are. Dearest scribe, write, be merry and be sure that this is the way of things, your way of things. Shrug off your dismal blanket, step out and enjoy the light. Dance and be merry for that is the way of things. Be sure that this is so and do not fret or worry or cast your concerns onto others. Be their light and their Beacon of trust and love from this day forward. Let them find you in the dark when they have lost their way and have little faith of finding their true path in the light.

For that is what you are, what you all are this day and forever and throughout time. Let all your lights shine and the Beacons of the World rise so that all may find their way and live in assurance that they are not alone, and will be guided with loving light to find their way, their path, with ease and with joy. Arise Beacons of the World, show yourselves and be seen so that all may see your lights and feel your presence and see that I am here with you and of you. Do not crowd like the flock of sheep waiting to be herded. Go forth and shine with love and confidence that this is the way. You are the way; we are the way of truth and light and love. And so be it. From this day on, may the world and Universe be lit by your love and ways. So be it.

Rest now, dear scribe, for the words have been many and the meanings more. Read this with delight and honour and love, for you are a Beacon for the world to see and honour. And others will follow as they feel the light opening their hearts with outpourings of love and joy. And be sure that it is so, always and forever. Now and forever and for all the past. The Universe dances in your love and grows with your light. Shine, dear Beacon, shine. Think on these words and be sure that as they are written so too do they appear in your heart and echo in the Universe, for it is so.

Read, remember, relax and shine so that others may see your glory, our glory, and follow you on your path. Leave your shrug, cover or blanket to one side. Open your heart, be still and be ready and shine for all to see. Rest now, dear scribe.

Please tell me more about Beacons and what this term means.

A Beacon is a pillar of light for all to see and move to. A Beacon is a pillar forged in love and light from the beginnings of time forward. A Beacon is not a perfect human but rather a perfect spirit who has reached the peak of their Earthly journeys and has agreed to perform this holy deed in the name of love, for all to see that your lives on Earth are but the blink of an eye for the Universe. What appears heavy or dull in Earthly terms is the golden key to untold joys that unfold like ripples in space with the weight of the task. They follow each other, hand in hand like lovers who cannot part or go separate ways. So too is the blessing of a trial that it may bring the joy of blessings immeasurable. Follow the ripple of joy, delight and know what I say to you is this: a Beacon brings all the light the world needs in one go, now and forever. For it was foretold at the beginning of time that Beacons, or pillars, would arise from the Earth when the darkness was heavy and blinded people to their true way or destiny. A Beacon holds the secrets of light and love in their hearts to rise up for all to see, to feel; and fear not for the ways of the Beacon are easy. They are simple, as light, love and believing are simple. There is no complicated formula or task to learn. Love, laugh and be merry; and be sure that your light will shine bright to bring others to their paths in joy and with a lightness that is bestowed upon them by the Universe, by all that there is and by me, by us, by each other. For as we are one, so shall our light and joy be one for all to be united in light, love and joy to dance and be merry, and dry the tears from their eyes and heavy hearts. Such is the nature of a Beacon.

Rise now all who have the light and love in their hearts and minds.

Cast no aspersion on those who rise up from the darkness, be sure that their strength is our strength, and your strength to be loved. Let it fill your hearts and minds and soul. Let your step be light and easy, do not falter as your way is clear for you to pursue. Be light of step and heart and follow in joy, for your life and ways will become easier as more blessings are given you with each passing day. And so it is. The darkness evaporates in the light of the sun and all things prosper in the light and rest in the dark. See yourselves as the seeds of time that open at the right moment with joy and glee and beauty untold. Feel the rise of joy as the light in your heart grows and waits gently for the ripe moment, your moment, our moment, to blossom and call forth the energies of the world from the darkness and their hidings. Spread your wings and fly. Rise like the mighty pillar that you are, so that all may feel your might and beauty and know it to be theirs too. This is the nature of the Beacon. Call forth all these energies and behold how your life will change.

Rest now, dear scribe, for we have spoken at length upon this subject. Rest now but summon the energies and light that are yours by divine right and decree. So be it. Let your way be lit with light and love, now and forever as foretold in the ages gone and in the Book of Time and your life. Be still now and be sure that this divine gift, nay, gifts, are yours, ours, to relish and enjoy. And so be it, now and forever, now and forever in our eternal moment.

Be still and love. Be your light. Call forth your energies; feel their power and watch in awe as your life transforms to radiate the light and love that becomes your being, your way and your path.

Arise Beacon of light, that others will see you shining brightly and follow in their own way with steps of joy. Be still now and rest and ponder on these words, as they take hold in your heart.

Are there already Beacons in the world?

Good morning, dear scribe, blessings and peace be upon you. You ask an important question for all need to know the nature of light and love and how it fills the world. This is but a frail thing, for many would seek to keep the darkness and all people in the shadows of their hollow glory. Be sure that when the time is right, the Earth will glow with the glory of those who rise to take their rightful place as pillars or Beacons. Be sure, too, that many know in their hearts that this is their divine calling and will rise as others too rise. Gentle scribe, there are already many Beacons who live their lives in love, with clarity and knowledge that this is the way forward. The dark is pierced by light, and hate dismantled by love. Be open to all that is new, for the signs are already there that you, we, and the world need this love and light now. Eons have passed since it was first spoken of and agreed by all that this will be the way forward, the only and true way. Many have already risen and more will arise like the birds of a flock who take flight as one from the snowy, barren Earth.

Be sure that this will be a moment of awakening and adjustment for the world, for us all. Be sure that it is so, and go about your days in peace knowing that this will be the way for all to love and laugh and be themselves in their true glory and destiny. Now when the time is heavy and dark, call forth your, our, Beacon strength and shine and love. And let all see that it is so and right. And so take flight, and others will follow in their own way at their own time. For it is so, now and forever. And it will echo through the voids and vastness of the Universe that light and love are once again on Earth as they were in the past, in days and ways now forgotten and swallowed in the ever-increasing pace of your, our, modern ways. For it was once known and whispered and talked about by all, and common knowledge for even the most innocent baby. Divine right and rights are bestowed on all for the glory of their lives, and to live in love. And so be it.

Is there much more to scribe?

Dearest scribe, you fret about time and wonder if your quill will be long enough. Do not; for the time, this time, will change all things and all things will change with ease and joy. Your scribing will last the right amount of time, for it was decreed in the opening of time that it would be so. Dear scribe, many will follow you and take up their mantle as Scribes to the Universe. Your role is but simple and will move forth with you in all your days. For it is so and has been agreed by all that we will speak of many things, so that all may understand the true nature of things; their true ways and selves. Let there be one long call for all to hear and follow, to rise and scribe and live their, our, lives in peace and love and the knowing that this is the way; the way of sharing and healing for all. Let the Universe light your way, our way, and steer the ship from the storm that would toss and destroy it. Be still, be happy and be sure that this is right and the way.

Rest now, dear scribe, and be sure that these words echo with love and joy throughout the Universe as one for all to see, hear and feel. The time is nigh and soon all will know of our words and deeds and find comfort that this is so, now and forever. Be still and rest, and be sure that soon all will know of this so that they, we, will join as one.

....
Thursday, 26 March 2020
....

What shall we talk about today?

Whatever you desire. What is the question your heart is aching to ask?

Why is it so hard to love, trust, and have faith in the goodness of people and the world without fear of loss or being hurt?

Dearest scribe, you ask so many beautiful questions. Fear arrives in your life like the unexpected visitor who slowly, step by step, gets deeper into your heart and home so that with time their presence is one with you and all that you cherish and love.

(The message seemed to stop here.)

How is it possible to love without fear on Earth?

My dearest scribe, your question is an important one and one in the hearts of many who feel in the dark but search for the light or the trusting foot to move on. And it is so, for life on Earth offers many options and fear is one of such choices. But it need not be so, for fear lives and dwells and delights in the mind and the imagination. For what could thoughts of fear be without the host of your mind and your very own co-operation? Where would fear then reside, were it not for the comforts of your own mind? Offer fear your best armchair and watch as it takes up residence in comfort. Feed it with thoughts of loss, of pain, of hurts and watch it grow like the glutton who can refuse no food. And it will swell and grow till it takes up residence in your heart and then your words and then your precious feelings and sentiments. When fear comes knocking at your door, do not entertain it or indulge it, for it to grow and grow. Be patient and tranquil, and know that all things come to pass, and so it is with any situation that you deem good or bad. And remember too, that fear is also your ally, your guardian who will warn you of darkness or 'errors' in your ways that may bring you to a situation that you do not relish. Fear may be your watchful friend with the lantern on your dark, lonely path, or the one who goads you and jibes at your every thought and action. Choose wisely for the choice is, and has been, always yours.

But trust that as you move forward every emotion has two sides, like a coin, and each side will bring its own blessings in its own unique way. Thus, fear may feel too much as a master when it is imbibed too

41

dearly and with too much attention. But in all things, it may serve you well as a reminder of your fragile human state. That is the beauty of fear, that it may serve you but only that. It is not your master nor should it ever be so.

Blessings and love are your divine right and nature, let fear appear only as your useful guide in your human world, but nothing more. Trust that to those who love, will love be their answer to all of life's woes, including fear itself. Do not wander into the darkness, the dreariness and heaviness of fear. Be light and be the light and let fear take its place — small and subdued.

(I stopped here as it all felt a bit unreal.)

Dearest scribe, do not doubt your ability to write my, our, words for they come from your, our, heart and are genuine and blessed. Rest now for we will speak of this again when you are rested and of a clearer mind. Be peaceful and happy, dear scribe, for all is well and will be well. Fear not, sparkles of light and Scribe to the Universe.

....

Saturday, 28 March 2020
....

In several of your messages, you spoke about the Book of Time. Can you tell me what it is?

Dear scribe, there are many who will question this reference and its true meaning. The Book of Time is one of the greatest books and wonders of the Universe and holds all the times and events that are of universal importance to you, us, all. A page that is marked, or open, signifies and shows an event that is momentous to us all for the greatness of the deeds it shows. The Book of Time is older than the Universe and time itself, for none could have created a greater or more magnificent creation than the Book of Time, which is ever open at your, our, page. So be it, gentle Scribe to the Universe, for the words are there for you, your understanding, and the greatness of your deed is in fact marked on your page in gold in the Book of Time. So be it. It is etched there for all to see and understand that our book of revelations and truths will soothe the hearts of the many who will take the meanings of our book to heart to hear the truth of life on planet Earth.

May it be so for all to see and understand this simple idea and truth that will set you all free from your daily toils and troubles. So be it. The Book of Time moves ever closer to you and your heart and the truth of it all.

Fret not, dearest one. Your time and glory is nigh, a time when all your dreams come true and love is your constant life companion. Rest now and rest assured that it is so, and ever was, and ever will be. In love, as always, Yahvay.

(I took a break after this short message and started typing up some of the notes.)

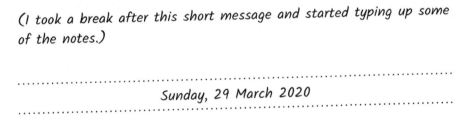

Sunday, 29 March 2020

Please tell me about death. Many loved ones are dying at the moment due to the coronavirus.

Dear scribe, write now for many are grieving and in search of answers. To all death is but a door, a portal if you will, from this world on. Death is but a transition from Earth form back to your original and only true form, that of loving spirit. Those who die do not disappear, for they cannot. No form can disappear or dissolve, the Universe knows no loss and all souls are accounted for and treasured this side and that. For it is necessary to remember that no one truly dies, that is not possible in spirit terms and the ways of the Universe. To all those who have lost and grieve, treasure the beauty and the wisdom of your loved ones, and know that they are ever yours for now and eternity. Your Earthly blindness obscures their love and presence, and know that they are ever with you for now and eternity. For love can never be truly lost or wasted or frittered away like Earthly time.

Love is all and all things are love, even if it appears otherwise. For those who have lost and are consumed with grief, be still and know that all is well. Your loved ones are but the blink of an eye away and tend to you and your needs every day, and every moment in every day. Your loved ones now reside in the Kingdom of Love where they are at peace and waking up from their Earthly dream. For that is the nature of life on Earth, 'tis but a dream finished in the blink of an eye and snuffed like a candle at the right time. There are no accidents or mishaps. The time, the moment, is always right and the release of a soul from its human body is a moment of joy, a time to rejoice and celebrate the passing of a frail soul. The wise and wizened know of this already and have done (so) for eons. Fret not, a soul's passing is a thing of beauty and not a thing to be bound by chains of grief and regret. Be joyous for the time shared and the time to be shared, for there is no loss, only transition.

Human emotions and lives limit the understanding of such a joyous event and time. Rest in its beauty and savour, nay, delight, at this joyous event. For though you cannot see or feel your loved one, be sure that they still speak to your heart in words and feelings of love. Be sure that this is so and never fret that it is otherwise, for that is not the case. Be sure, scribe, that you have conveyed this well and that it will bring comfort to those who weep and wail for they know no peace. Be sure that all things pass, and so too will the darkness left after the sorely, missed loved one's life has been transmuted, changed and referred back to the realm and remit of spirit. And so it is, that all things always change in the sacred cycle of love, life, and death on Earth. For it is so, and always has been so, and will always be so, for this is the eternal plan, the eternal way of all things for all things. Things that come and go, come and go. Are here, then not. Are there, then not. 'Tis is the way of all things and all people.

So, weep no more for your lost ones, for they are never truly lost, only moved to a new residence in a new world and life. Suffer not the little ones, for their loss is the greatest, but also the sweetest in terms of souls returning for the briefest of time on Earth. Such a departure after such a short stay was ordained and agreed by all souls who have love in this situation. Their lessons are great and gilded in love by love itself. These are the giants of the soul world whose love is like a tsunami, rushing forth and engulfing all in its path. There is no stone unturned, no soul forgotten or lost. Only love and more love. For this is the way of love and darkness, of love and darkness.

Be sure to speak these words as they appear on your page for the comfort of those in the throes of loss and grief. Let it open the door to light and love, so that they too may live the joy and elation of those departed. For those who grieve and dwell on the loss see not how perfect it all is, has been, and will be for now and forever. Let their hearts lighten with joy and understanding that no soul, no person is ever truly lost, only moved to a different realm to keep watch over those left on the Earth plane, the loved ones left behind. For the bonds of true love cannot, and are not, ever truly broken. They cannot be, for this is impossible. No such act is ever considered, as love is supreme and cannot be lost or destroyed or broken. Such is the divine way, the way of all things now and forever, now and forever.

Rest, dear scribe, for we have spoken at length on a sore topic. Rest and be sure that these words are true and truest for those who have need of them, now and forever, now and forever. Rest and go your way in gentleness and peace for none can touch you or your dignity. Be sure of this and raise the torch, your torch, our torch, higher for all to see and believe in.

So be it, gentle scribe. Go your way in peace and happiness for all that you do and all those that you help. So be it. Rest now.

APRIL

The days are starting to get longer, which is always so welcome if you live in northern countries like the UK. The winter cold and darkness are hard for most people, so longer days with their increased daylight nurture the promise of the long summer days filled with sunshine and warmth.

This year, the lockdown continues in the UK and many other European countries. Sadly, the death toll continues to rise daily. I now try not to watch the news as it is so sad and sometimes very upsetting. It's better to live in my own world of scribing and typing it up; safe in my home away from the world and all its bad news.

This month I got an external validation that my diary is not a waste of time or a flight of fantasy. This means so much to me, for although I have been encouraged many times during the messages, how could I guarantee it was not just wishful thinking? A figment of my imagination? I have now finished typing up all the words, so far 17,241 words, including the most recent conversations! I did wonder at the start of the typing if it would come to 5,000 words, then maybe 10,000, then perhaps 15,000; after that, I kept excitedly checking the final word count and started printing the pages to edit and check.

It's now the end of April and I have filled my first notebook! Next month I will have another almost new notebook to fill.

I'm now starting to get excited, really excited, about the possibility of publishing a book — a real book! And by me! Okay, well, us!!

I also generally feel happier, more relaxed, and less buffeted by life's little 'treats'. I find I laugh more and generally feel that there's more of a personal purpose to my life — something quite new and novel for me.

My sleep is improving! After years of erratic sleep — too little or too much — or not being able to fall asleep, my sleeping is now more regular. It's so much better. I now often fall asleep faster, sleep better, and even wake up feeling refreshed some mornings. What a novelty!

We reunite, dear Yahvay! Please help me to understand. Earlier you said that you are a creator but not The Creator. You said I can call you 'The One', but some people refer to God as 'The One'. Is there more than one God, or did God not create all things as many people believe?

Dearest gentle scribe, you are right to ask this important question for it will perplex many people. You rightly say that I told you I am not The Creator for there are many angels and beings that support me in all I do. I am The One, The Creator of all that is beautiful and fine, and all that is dark and confusing, of all that is light and dark, heavy and light. For how can you choose if the options are not there? How can you ask for black shoes if only brown ones are all you can find?

(I found this writing difficult and had to keep stopping.)

Clear your mind, gentle scribe, for the words are there, but you cannot hear them.

In all things am I, and all things are me, for I am The Creator of all that is and ever will be. We are one as always, as all-time has shown and will show. There is no force other than me, I am the essence of all, all that is good and bountiful and all that is not good — for I cannot be one and not the other. I cannot be the light and not be the dark. I cannot be love without being hate. Such is the nature of all things on Earth and in the Universe, for I cannot be one thing without being the other. Remember all things are me, even in your darkest hour I am there, for how can I be one thing and not the other? Can you have only one side of a coin? In the darkest place in space, am I not there? In the most joyful of moments, am I not there? Whispers in your ear and heart are the call of the Universe, of me, of my angels and of my realm. Be still and feel the words coming and their meanings will unfold for you to understand. Creation was my will for all time and for all ways. The stars in the night sky sparkle their love to you, the wind that rushes is my love for all, and even if it destroys, recall that it is the force of my love for all things that brings such energy to bear. For all things are me and I am in all things.

(I stopped here as it felt very difficult to hear the words and I had to keep pausing.)

Friday, 3 April 2020

Dearest Yahvay, I found yesterday's message difficult to write, as I have on some other occasions. I can't always hear the words well and sometimes I doubt that what I'm writing is correct. Please tell me your thoughts on this.

Dear scribe, you hesitate and doubt, but all is well. We 'talk' this way as it is easiest for you, and you are able to channel my words and meanings well. Do not fret, for no false words have been written or scribed. You hear me well, see and feel my meanings. Remember I told you that great deeds are done in stillness, in peace and in quiet. So, it is with you. Quieten your mind, put to one side the ideas of your daily tasks and toil, they will wait and be done at the right time when all that is necessary has been completed.

Rest now for your shoulder pains you. Resume when you are comfortable.

Yahvay, please help me with my shoulder.

(There followed a mini-meditation; I felt tingles and energy in my body. I now feel more relaxed, there's less pain and I can even write faster!)

Thank you, Yahvay, that was wonderful.

Dear scribe, as we move forward the writing and the messages will become easier for you to follow. Suffice it to say, that as we go deeper into our union and communion, you will write more with more clarity, and less feeling of doubts that, like clouds, float into your mind and obscure the sun and your vision and understanding. Suffice it to say also, that time itself will bend and wander and slow so that all of this will be done in the blink of an eye. A wondrous feat in Earth terms, for many see their time as a line from A to B only, with no variation or change to the speed of the distance covered. Remember time is your illusion, your guard who dictates your movement and freedom. There is no key for a quick release when you see time as ongoing in its straight line. It is not your red bus with its limited stops and only allowing a few people to ascend or descend.

You are all masters of time and its manipulation, for that is the trickery of the illusion; it will keep you spellbound without you realising that you have the power, the mighty power, to change it at your will. The clock face moves in direct relation to your expectations of how the hands should move — fast or slowly. This is the illusion that all submit to, without realising their folly and the folly of it all. Bend time now to suit you. You are the owner, the holder of this gift, nay, this divine right. Do not submit to the idea that time is fixed and only in one place. Its bounds are limitless and nothing at the same time. It is the spiral that takes you with it, ever inward, ever outward, ever up, ever down. It is a trickster that will have you follow its lead. Be done with it and its rigours, its constraints, for it will take you where it will. Fear not, for the illusion of time, though subversive, need not carry you at all times and in all ways. Let the flow stop, be still in silence, for time will wait and answer your call, your beckoning, your summoning. Relish this 'time' as one of great discovery for you and all those who would understand the true nature of reality.

The darkness of space, the Universe, has its own time and ways of operating, yet you still measure it and understand it through the folly of (Earth) time. No such creation would ever be subjected to such rigours or waste; for the folly of time is but a waste and an academic study alone. Be done with the need to measure everything with the lens of time as your guide. It serves you not. Be done with it. And so, dear scribe, finish here for we have spoken at length on this topic.

Rest and go about your day in peace and joy, and live your life in love for that is your natural state and your divine gift to share with all. Be done now.

Peace and blessings be yours now and forever. Peace and blessings.

....
Sunday, 5 April 2020
....

Good morning, Yahvay, on this beautiful, sunny day. There are a few more questions I would like to ask you, but would it be better if you dictated or said what you think is important for people to know?

Dearest scribe, sink into the well of tranquillity. You will ask the right questions for I will guide your thoughts and heart. Many will want to hear the questions you ask as they have wondered the same themselves. Your questions are more important at present as they are your heart's desire, and thus the desire of many on Earth. Please ask your next question, for it is an important one.

You know?

Of course, I thought of it first.

(I had to stop at this point because I was laughing so much! I'd believed that I had thought of all the questions, when nothing was further from the truth!)

Before you, what was there?

There was a nothing, a nothing so complete it filled the Universe and all reaches of time with nothing. For there was no Universe, no time, a total nothing except for the force of love, me. That is how I came into being, a drop at a time into the ocean of love that we call the Universe and time. The echoes of this love still reverberate throughout time and the Universe, for how can it be otherwise? How can a nothing, a total nothing, become something if it were not for the energy of love? Such a force has, and can create all; the planets, stars and suns. Such is the force and the power of love. Eternal beings are made of the dust of stars, the galactic clouds and the tears of love that fall as rain on the Earth. Why so would it be otherwise? How so could it be different? All thoughts of love bring peace and power to this creation, a creation fashioned eons ago with the essence of love at its core. Behold the stars at night and wonder why they twinkle so. For is it not the same every night that you gaze at the beautiful, black, night sky? These essences — stars — are there for your love and delight for they were forged, nay, hewn, out of the stone of love. As the ocean of love grows, drop by drop, day by day, let all know the truth of reality. Drop by drop will their own lives grow and flourish like the seas of the Universe. So be it.

Eons will pass before this message is fully understood and equated on Earth, for this is a trying muddle of all that is good and all that is not good. Angels of mine guard and watch over the weak, the poor and the infirmed. Day and night, night and day. For did I not create the sun with its immense force to sustain your life on Earth? Did I not create the fauna, the trees, the winds and the rain for your sustenance and delight? All this and more was created in, and by, the name of love. Love is all there is and love is supreme. The king, if you will, or the queen. Let all things remain supreme in the glory of their being, and the light of their eminence.

Rest now, for you tire and struggle with the words. We are here and will write again soon — the morrow if you will, and it pleases you. Rest now, gentle scribe, and be satisfied that today you asked an important question, and one that needed to be asked and explained.

Go about your day in love and remember the words we have shared, for they are mighty and greater than the simple pen that fashioned them. Let it be so, and go about your day in love and delight as more unfolds for the delight of all those who will read these words and ponder, nay, wonder at their truth. So be it, gentle scribe. Rest and gorge yourself on the feast of knowledge we share at this important time on Earth. Till the morrow, be still, be quiet, be happy.

Wednesday, 8 April 2020

Good morning, Yahvay, on this beautiful sunny day. I have a more personal question that I'd like to ask today. Why do I live so much of my life in fear or anxiety?

Dearest scribe, be still and listen. Listen well and heed these words. In silence and death come euphoria, in all else is doubt; always a choice — is this right or that? Should I do this or that? Ever going and ever rushing fills your time, your days, your life with dread. How can I manage it all? And all alone? This is the sentiment of your modern 'civilised' life. Always running, always choosing. Has it not all become too much? Ever too much? Slow to an amble, nay, a dawdle, and saunter your way along life's path. For how can you love and understand who you truly are with the visor of haste always filtering your thoughts and feelings? How can you understand the nature of your reality if it is so finely held by the threads of haste and worry?

You know not who you truly are, your true magnificence, your glorious past and future all lost in the dust of speed. Like the dust scattered by the galloping horse's hooves. Stop now with this idiocy of running, running and running. Hang up the running shoes, the keys to the car and stop. Be still and silent and feel the love around you, like the arms of a mother comforting her dearest child. Be sure that those arms comfort you now, for are you not beloved? Remember this is the truth of us, all of us. For how can it be otherwise? Go about your days in the

56

peace and knowledge that it is so. It cannot be otherwise. Remember that all who love are always loved in return.

Those who fear, as you do, live too deeply in the illusions of your modern life and world. Do not believe that it is so, for your modern life parades many wonders for your delight, but they are fleeting and the joy fades. These modern wonders will all fade as time passes and dictates their demise. Be not spellbound or in awe at these modern ways, for they take you backwards and move you further from your true delights and joy of being who you are, who you truly are and all that you already have. Do not let your mind and imagination concoct its very own and very personal theatre of doom just for you. Do not enter this theatre, nor even buy the ticket to witness this spectacle of doom. Such are the wonders all around you, all already there waiting for your delight and joy at their discovery. Behold these wonders and close your private theatre of art macabre, refuse the dark mask and smile in joy and comfort, knowing you are so truly loved. Now and always. Then and always. For once started, the machinations of love do not falter or veer away on a new course.

Be still, know that it is so in your heart, not in your head — that thinking box that cannot stop and knows no bounds. Feel all with your heart and be sure that you are right, for did I not endow you with these wondrous gifts and a love deeper than you can imagine? Believe it to be so, now and forever, now and forever.

Fare well, dear scribe, for we have discussed your point and shared its meaning. So be it. Farewell. Till the morrow. Love, light and joy be yours, now and forever. Now and forever.

....
Friday, 10 April 2020
....

Dearest Yahvay, good morning to you! I would like to ask you a more personal question again, please. Why am I so terrified of dealing with Saul? (This is a pseudonym for someone I had dealt with for years, but things were turning out to be potentially unpleasant.)

Your fear overwhelms you like the rising waves in a storm. Be still and realise that all is not as it seems, for you have right on your side. Believe this and move forward with integrity and fairness, and love and bliss in your heart for none can touch you — immortal spirit and warrior that you are.

Remember the theatre of gloom and histrionics? Do not go there, much as it entices you in. You have been there many times in the past and would re-enter now, but there is no need. Close the door to this place and reside more in the green of nature with its calming effects. Stay by the stream in your mind *(I saw a beautiful, peaceful stream, with trees and grassy banks in my mind)* and let it not become the torrent or storm that you fear. Take heart, brave one, for none can touch you, no matter how they may shout or strut. Let calmness, love and assuredness be yours now and forever, now and forever. Breathe in your calm and be at peace, now and forever. Till the morrow, rest, dearest one, and enjoy the unfolding of joy and pleasure in your day.

Thank you so much! I do indeed feel a lot calmer now. Why did I, or we, agree that I would become 'Scribe to the Universe'?

Eons have passed and you cannot now remember your ecstasy at taking on this mantle, this role. Such a role was destined to be yours, but not yours alone, at this time of changes on Earth.

Your words, our words, will bring comfort to millions by the written word or the words of friends who relate the book to others. The role of scribe is an important one and not one to be taken lightly, for many would have the title but not wear the mantle with responsibility. Your role as 'Scribe to the Universe' was chosen for you as love and gentleness fill your heart, and you wonder at the glory of it all. 'Scribe to the Universe', have you not recalled the sacred moment the seal was made? Our pact? Our agreement? You are a messenger for us all in the eternal realm.

Your pen grows still as you cannot hear me. Let us resume the morrow. Be in peace, gentle scribe. Light, love and blessings be yours, and go about your day thus.

Rest for now and delight in all the joys the day will bring you. Till the morrow. Peace, light and love be yours to share with a smile to those who most need it.

· ·

Easter Sunday, 12 April 2020

· ·

Happy Easter, Yahvay. Easter is a reminder of the death of your son, and all that it meant for the world. Today I thought of asking you about people who are chronically or seriously ill. It seems unfair that people may suffer like this. Please let me know your thoughts.

There are moments, and they are only moments for the Universe, when things must stop to be re-adjusted. This course is not due to lack or error but by design for the blessings of strength, courage, beliefs and time to dwell and grow and flourish in stillness. Such is the design of all great things that many deem wrong or a disaster. Such times are blessings in the joys and gifts hidden in the dark and blackness of it all. So too are their *(people who are ill)* days passed in silence and gratitude that all will pass, and the joy of spring after the dark winter will once again lighten the days with celebration and joy. Accept all with patience and delight in the knowledge of all it offers, like the box of treasures to be opened with the key of patience and forbearance.

(I was starting to feel selfish for not asking about Jesus' death at Easter and had launched straight into my question without any reference to this, instead of asking how this may have affected Yahvay.)

So be it, for today you struggle and stumble on my words and your thoughts of what you have not asked, and I thank you for your thoughts of love — a mother's love and consideration for what the father may feel. The anguish and desolation of a son so brutally and cruelly murdered was to be felt and experienced but not to be dwelt on, for that was not the design nor the purpose of such an act.

Designs may be yours or mine, but the results are always ours to cherish and learn by. Such is the school of life on Earth in all its ambiguities and nuances, its shades of meaning and doubt. For the strongest grow tall and the weakest honoured in their humility and smallness.

Ripples of cause and effect travel the Universe in its vastness and entirety, so that all may learn and feel for those who have designed their own cells of darkness and despair. Open the door, the box, and let the light in, for you all possess the keys of self-knowledge and the wisdom of the ages. Align with this and hold your key close to your heart that knows all secrets — whispered or not. The wind changes course to deliver the goodness of time to all those who listen. Stop and listen to the secrets of the wind and feel your heart grow in the certainty that all is well.

Stop now, scribe, for you tire and struggle with the words. The morrow is full of promise and delight and let us meet there. For now, stop and be happy at the words you have written, the meanings and understanding you have received, for this is your blessed way, and the blessed way of many who feel this plight. Take heart and be light. Be your love and happiness, now and forever. Peace and blessings be yours today and forever.

Till the morrow, dearest scribe. Rest now, for you have written much.

Good morning, dear Yahvay. Thank you for being with me and for all the messages you have sent and send whenever I ask. I was typing up more of our 'discussions' and came across the term — or idea — of calling forth my strength. What is the best way to do this?

Dearest scribe, I bless you and all who read these words. May you live in light and love.

To call forth your strength, be still. In Earth terms this may be to meditate, to dream; but to stop your frantic day to day rushing and clear your mind so that it is the blank canvas and space for spirit to reach you, to paint the words and pictures you need that will help you, and move you forward in whatever quest you have chosen or whatever trial you now face.

It is enough to breathe deeply in this space for that is the signal that spirit is invited into your space and life. Healing can then occur; wisdom and strength restored to your original glory. In such a space command that your strength be restored and see it, for it will happen according to your desires and the truth of Universal laws. Your wholeness is but a breath away, but is dictated by your volition and requests. Be still and be sure that this is the truth, that all may use and benefit from. Stillness and demanding are the keys to your success. Though you see it or not, be sure that such a process, once begun, will take place. Do so with love and gentleness for yourself and all others in your life for we are all of one family and one time, now and forever.

Be still, gentle scribe, and know that all is well and exactly as it should be, the way it was planned and foretold in the ages that have turned to dust and forgotten in the hurry of your, our, modern life.

So be it. For today that is all I have to say. Use this time and silence to make yourself whole again so that you may better move forward in

61

light and with success in all that you do and dream of doing.

So be it, gentle scribe, till the morrow. And yes, type our conversations up as we go along — in our merry way.

. . . .

Wednesday, 15 April 2020

. . . .

Dearest Yahvay, when you say 'command', what is the best way to do this? Will it not be seen as rude to command? And more to the point, do humans have the power or right to command things?

Gentle scribe, good morning. Peace and blessings be yours on this beautiful day. You are early this morning.

To command is a right bestowed on all humans when it is for a just cause and without harm to others. For if it fits your plan of life, so be it. It cannot be seen as rude, for spirit and the Universe have no judgement on your actions. To command, simply say that you command and the event you so desire. But remember a command must be heartfelt, and better still that it helps or aids others. When the task of the command is big in your eyes you may feel resistance in your heart, for you have been taught and schooled in the thought that only those who are deserving may ask, and only those who are pure of heart may receive. This is not so, for all humans have the divine right to call and command the energies of the Universe, for are we all not one? How could it be for me to be able to decide and command certain things and you not? If we are all one, this has no sense or meaning.

Command to your heart's desire and only that, for commands that would hurt others cannot be fulfilled. It is but simple to command, and yet humans in their ever fretful and hurried lives rush past this divine option, this fork in the road that would serve as their short cut to what their heart desires and would dictate. For that is the true nature of our union, that I may speak to your heart in the language of love. Follow its desires in peace and love. So much has been lost, or buried, only to be rediscovered like some ancient treasure.

Be still now and voice your commands that they may better your life and the lives of others. Do so soon with love and gentleness and a knowing gratitude of your awakening and re-finding of your true gifts and nature. Go now, light the candle on your altar and command that your strength be restored and that your true nature and gifts be revealed this day and all days forth.

So be it. Rest now, remember and use this knowledge and we will speak again on the morrow.

Peace and blessings be yours and may love light your way, now and forever blessed one, blessed scribe.

....

Thursday, 16 April 2020

....

Dearest Yahvay, good morning to you on this beautiful day! Yesterday after we had finished, I heard more words to complete some of the things you had said. Sometimes when I type up what I've written, it doesn't make sense to me. Am I hearing you properly?

Dearest scribe, you are doing an important task well, for these words will bring comfort to many as they bring comfort to you now. There are times when your mind is not clear or still and so you struggle to hear all that I say — like just now. You write words of wisdom and with faith that all that I say is right and just; for you have your own ideas of God and what such an entity should be like. Therefore, sometimes your heart will *(wants to)* dictate or try to dictate your own version of my truth. Fear not, scribe, for we are at but the early days of our venture, and as time passes, so too will the clarity and ease with which you hear me improve and increase.

Be still for me to talk to you and clear your mind of your own ideas. You think that I communicate with you only when you scribe, but that is not so, for are we not one and always in communion? And so it is that in your daily tasks be still and listen, for I speak to you always, and always in tones of love. Listen now and be sure that what you hear are indeed my words, now and forever. For it has always been so and always will be in the eternity of time that we call the Universe. Be still and scribe and be sure that you write well and with accuracy, for being a 'Scribe to the Universe' is a heavy mantle that not all would take lightly.

Go about your day now, in peace and love and so be it, scribe. Light up the world with your words and love, for you are a Beacon rising to shine in dark times for humans on Earth. Let the world shine with you and let others know so that they too may take up their pens, their quills, and scribe as you do. Have faith, dearest scribe, that what you are doing is right and just, and important for others who will follow your lead and example.

Rest now for we have spoken at length on the topic. Be sure and have faith and be happy in your luck and good fortune. So be it. Days of glory be yours now and forever, dear scribe.

Till the morrow when you take up your quill again. Love, peace and blessings be yours.

. . . .

Friday, 17 April 2020

. . . .

Dearest Yahvay, peace and blessings be ours on this beautiful day. Today I would like to discuss your point about the pain of a father that you talked about on Easter Sunday. Are you a father? Are you male?

Dearest scribe, you raise an important point and I thank you for doing so. Many have asked the same question and many continue to ask now. For am I not the father of all creation? But the mother too. For it is the mother that creates and gives birth to new creations on Earth. This is a way, one way, and the way on Earth. For me to be one with you I must be female, but for me to be one with a man I must be male — in Earth terms. But how could that be so? Would I need to change from female to male and vice versa to suit Earth needs and comprehension? What a limiting idea bound by the apparent truth of your life and understanding dictated by your life on Earth. This simplistic binary division exists not in spirit, what use would we have of gender? To procreate? On Earth, you manage that all on your own without our support.

The sorrow of a father is as deep as that of a mother; almost. For a mother feels the loss of part of her as she loses a child. This pain cuts deep and some never recover to regain their full glory in life on Earth. The loss for a father cuts deep too, and it is for this that I said so. For many will identify with Jesus as my son, but can that really be so? Yes, I am the father and yes, I am the mother; for how could I be one and not the other? Like the two sides of a coin, I am one and both at the same time. For I am your father and your mother in Earth terms and understanding; but in truth, I am both and neither. How could a divine, eternal being be confined to one name, one label? I am a creator, The Creator, of all that is, and do so not in the ways of Earth and its limited ways and thinking.

But you referred to yourself as the father, please help me understand this point.

Dear scribe, your ideas can block your writing and my message. Patience in all things is often the wisest of counsels.

I referred to the pain of a father whose son was brutally murdered as this is the truth and the way, for I am the 'father' and the 'mother' as I am The Creator of all. Here we have a problem with a name, a label. But for a divine being no such names or labels are necessary, for what is, is, and what has been, has been. Experience dictates the need to follow through on certain actions and ideas, but the feelings lie dormant, waiting like the seeds in the tilled, dark field of earth. A seed sprouts but does not ask the origin of its creation. It grows and blossoms and rejoices in its life — brief though it may be. So too with people, who spring to life and do not know the true origin of their creation, ever, on Earth.

So, with names and labels be done, for they serve little purpose other than on Earth for your ease of reference. Such a trivial pursuit holds little value in the Universe and the Realm of Spirit, the realm of all that has been and ever will be. Here the true currency is feeling and love, love above all.

And so, with the use of the word or name 'father', would it have made more sense and jarred less if I had said 'creator'? And in place of 'son' put 'creation'? For that is the true nature of it, and the truth that pervades life on Earth in all its glory, for there are too many dark days when the loss of my creation cuts deep — and deeper than you can imagine. For so it is in love and light, and dark and loss. 'Father', 'mother' are but Earth names for creators as it is on planet Earth.

So be it. Rest now, dear scribe, and have faith that these words are true and will bring comfort and understanding to many, for that is the nature of our discourse. Let it be so, and arise in pride for what you achieve in the name of love and the glory of God; your glory too. For as you scribe these words, all will understand better the true nature of their reality as it is on Earth.

Rest now, dear scribe. Ponder on these words and understand their meaning with your heart, not your mind that would wander of its own accord and volition and come full circle without achieving what it wanted; a restless understanding of a world dictated by rules or logic and numbers. Such a false understanding and way of being.

Rest now, and be sure that what you write is accurate and much needed. Till the morrow, dearest scribe. Love, peace and blessings be yours, ours.

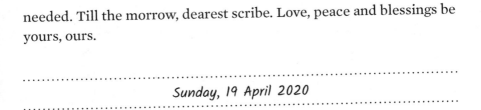

Dearest Yahvay, peace, blessings and happiness be ours, and good morning to you. As we are now writing a book for others to read, is it alright to include personal questions? Or should I only ask about global issues?

Dearest scribe, you will always ask the 'right' question for we formulate the questions together, for where would I be without you, 'Scribe to the Universe'? And where would you be without me? This union forged in love was decreed and had design eons ago with the scope of letting the world know of its contents. As such, whatever question you may pose will be 'right' and just, for how could it be otherwise? Your personal questions must be voiced, aired, for they have the answers your heart yearns to hear. And not yours alone, for are we all not one? Mother of sadness that would hold you in its mist of darkness and despair, you are not alone. For you imagine not that others may too find themselves in your dark, lonely place. This is not the truth, nor ever can be for we are all one, now and forever.

Ask the questions that your heart burns with desire to hear the answers to, for they are the most pressing of matters. In all things, your heart will, and should, dictate your actions and ideas. Your task is to follow its lead, hear its voice, for all will be well then. Trials and tribulations may be the order of the day, but fear not for all is balanced and considered and the end result just. So too are the scales of justice, for they balance in an equal way, in equal measure, the weight of the deeds placed on one part will necessitate the weight of the result on the other part. The result, if you will. Justice, words and deeds are never lost in isolation, but always tied and bound together with your thoughts and volition and spirit. As you would ask about yourself, the words are placed on one side for all to see, read and feel. The answer is placed on the other side for all to see and justice — eternal justice — be done. For as you ask about yourself, you ask about others, and as you hear your reply, so too do others. Therefore, no personal question can exist, for if you ask about yourself, what your heart feels or fears, so do you ask and express the feelings of others' hearts. And mine too.

There are no global issues which are not also affairs of the heart. How can that be so? Your concern and fear at the destruction, and sadness at the loss of all that is beautiful and bountiful is shared by all. Even those who destroy and lust after the trophy of winning, of prestige, of power, so too do they feel it in their hearts — hearts that are silenced in the name of greed and a lust of destruction and a feeling that they are gods to do as they please. Who on planet Earth can raise their hand to claim their innocence in this? To 100%? For it is not possible to live on Earth and not be guilty as charged in the rape and destruction of your beautiful, precious gift: the Earth. No question on the global scale excludes you, dear scribe, just as no personal question excludes the rest of the world. That cannot be so, for are we all not one?

Take the sadness that you feel at the revelation of this truth, nurture it and let it be the spur that jars you and others into action, an army of love to march and shout and defend the rights of your mother — Mother Earth — for she needs your support and love and respect now and every day. In the past and into the eternal future, all now and now.

So be it, scribe. Your question, our question, was a 'good' one and worthy of asking. The answer has been long but illuminating. Read it with your heart, not out of guilt, but with love and understanding of its message for you and all on Earth — that gem in the Universe. Love and tenderness are the Earth's needs, do this and watch her, and you flourish in your togetherness of love and respect.

So be it, scribe. Rest now, for the day and the morrow bring us both delights to share. Till the morrow, gentle scribe. Peace, love and blessings be yours, ours, for the Universe to witness and note. So mote it be.

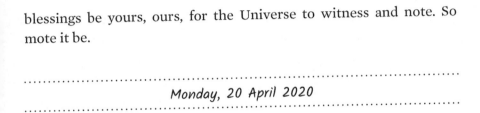

Good morning to you, dearest, on this beautiful day. Today I would like to ask you about trees and flowers. Do they have feelings, such as happiness? Can they communicate with each other?

My dearest scribe, your question today, though seemingly trivial to some, is an important one. For as I said earlier, all things on planet Earth are sentient, that includes all the living things in your garden, a park or in the vast forests of the world. They live in harmony with each other, though some may seem more adept at taking their space, growing profusely. They have a will to grow where they are best suited for themselves, and not for the ways of people.

The songs of the Universe echo in their space and the knowledge of the ages is stored in the deepest woodlands and forests, and in the oldest of trees. Those who know and can understand this already listen to this voice and hear, or feel, this harmony that silently knits its members together in joy. They do not fear, as they have nought to fear, all is given to them in abundance. Leaves that whisper and flowers bold in their colours delight in the joy of each new day. They sing the song of creation and know not of the desire to cull and cut and destroy. For each plant grows at will from the design of a tiny seed, a gem of creation and a master plan — the blueprint of nature that allows all to fit together in harmony and joy. For what purpose is there in plants and flowers that are dull and bring no joy to the eye — the beholder?

The grass, flowers, trees and shrubs can each sense each other, and understand their own needs for space and for light. Many will wane and wilt, placed in the wrong space with the wrong intentions, for they are all able to sense your joy or anger or otherwise. They know the moon, the sun and the stars, and relish the rain sent to aid their growth and beauty. They sense, too, the goodness of the gardener, and the volitions or intent of that person, and each person who would spend time in their company.

Cutting, pruning and the destruction of trees is a blight, a blackspot on planet Earth, for the green gives bounty and life, which is not to be destroyed wantonly or through malice and greed. Nature in all her forms senses this imbalance, and tears of rain deluge the areas not bound by joy or love. Such is the nature of the verdant nature on planet Earth. That all things be respected and loved is necessary to preserve the oft precarious balance that works in perfect harmony, with no aid needed from man or humans. The Earth will prosper and offer her gifts in bounty when all the planet, even the tiniest 'weed', is treated with respect and reverence for the beauty of each creation.

Rest now, scribe, for we will discuss more on nature in the morrow. Till then, rest, be happy, and love and respect each perfect creation offered to you in joy and love by nature in all her wondrous bounty.

Till the morrow, rest, be happy and behold the beauty all around you offered in love, simply love.

Till the morrow dearest, scribe. Love, laugh and be happy.

. . . .

Wednesday, 22 April 2020

. . . .

Good morning to you, dearest Yahvay, on this beautiful day. Please tell me more about nature and the welfare of animals in the world.

Good morning to you, dearest scribe. Such is our discourse on nature that we must also consider the well-being of all sentient creations, which necessitates a discourse on the plight of the Earth's animals —

suffering as they are. Human actions generate disaster in many areas: the land, the skies, the seas. Even the very sun would be blighted if possible.

Your actions, all of your actions, including yours, dearest scribe, do not ever really consider the plight, or otherwise, of your natural neighbours and the bountiful lands you all live in. Such is the haste and growth of humans that nature has no respite from the onslaught of modern machines and ways. Always more and more, and ever faster. You, humans, know no bounds, for they interest you little or not at all. There is no respect for the greenness of the valley, the silver rains that fall, or your verdant, beautiful world filled with the colour of birdsong. All brushed to one side, flattened and destroyed in your avarice and greed. Stop now, for the eternal clock has sounded to decree that all is not right or fair in these ways. Your ever longing for more will run the rivers dry, mar your seas and oceans, and poison the very air that you would breathe. Can this be right? This ever-frantic game where all players, all players, are involved is the very key to its destruction; your destruction and demise are ensured. For how will you live when the rivers are dry, the Earth arid and barren, and your very air a poison to your body? It must stop before you end the game, unwittingly or otherwise.

Pause now and think of it all. The machinations of modern ways bear little or no respect for the gifts you were so graciously given, the natural bounty of life on Earth — the blue gem of the Universe. Stop now, pause and reflect on your modern ways and all that is necessary for them. Your conveniences and comforts all cost, for that is the way of things. Ever larger is the human number, and ever greater the impact on Earth and Mother Nature. How long will you play this game? This dicing with death and destruction? Roll the dice for a 6 and think you have won, you get another go, but there is always a cost, an ever-amounting cost, for nature and you all. Roll the dice and consider 1 the best number, not more, not less, but 1, for that is what we all are: 1; 1 with creation and 1 with love, patience and adoration for all that is granted and given for your joy and abundance each new day. But strip this bare in greed and haste, pillage all for your own needs, and watch as your home dies. The demise of a beautiful and bountiful world is on you all. Even the most innocent of babies has a role in the game, a deadly game for your world and Mother Nature and all the gifts and bounty she would offer you. And who then will bury the Earth in its sacred grave?

So too do all your animals suffer. Some showered in love, others beaten and starved, and still others hunted mercilessly for the 'bounty' they offer. What a game. Can it really be just? And such is the plight of many, many animals on Earth, who would but live their lives according to the natural ways, not the ways of humans, always designed for gain and for more, yet more. Light the candle of hope and let its glow allow you to see clearly. For in the darkness do you fumble and grab and grab. Believe in your light and the light of love for all sentient creations — animals or otherwise — and leave them be. Take only what is yours by right, not in greed or the desire to destroy. The Earth weeps at your wanton brutality, the gaping scars on her face and the destruction of all that is beautiful and natural. The Earth and human life are not a good match, they go not well together.

Such is the frantic greed of this human species that nought can withstand its onslaught. Like busy ants always scurrying but always destroying. Peace and tolerance and patience all pushed to one side in the modern haste of modern life. Stop now, for the river runs dry, the rains do not fall and all will perish in the barrenness of it all. Your toxic ways and waste poison your very home, and you may no longer open the window in search of clean air, for what is there is but worse than what you already have. Stop, breathe, and wait. Wait for your answers from within, for they will be right and just. Look not at your neighbour except in love. The lust and desire of more bring you down, you all down. Respect and love your world, your precious beautiful world, and wonder not if the sun will rise or if the moon and stars will grace your skies in their beauty. For all things, there is a cycle, a natural cycle and a wonderment to it all. Take this wonder and treasure it, hold it close and custody it. It is your treasure, your wonder, your delight and your right to live in bounty and love.

Clean the seas, the oceans, the airs, and watch how nature replenishes all for your delight and nourishment. Take and take and spoil, and watch how your time on Earth is ever shorter and ever with lack. For lust with no bounds destroys all in its path. Be slow, be gentle and be patient, for they are the ways of bounty and plenty for all to share, enjoy and love.

So be it, gentle scribe. You have risen early to write much and it is good for we have spoken at length on this topic.

Rest now and ponder on the truth of these words, for the blight and plight of the Earth is on you all, on you all. Rest now and go about your day in light and love, and blessings be yours to enjoy and relish in.

Till the morrow, dearest gentle scribe. Be pleased for you have written much and well.

· ·

Thursday, 23 April 2020

· ·

(Many years ago, I heard about a tree surgeon who stopped working on trees as he said he could hear them screaming as he cut them. This prompted today's question.)

Good morning to you, dearest Yahvay, on this wonderful day. Today I would like to cut back some shrubs and trees in the garden, but I often wonder if they feel pain when we do this. Is this a daft idea?

Good morning to you, dearest scribe. You ask about the trees and shrubs in your garden and you are right to do so, for many ignore these sentient beings either through volition or, as is often the case, through ignorance. As I said before, all things on planet Earth are sentient; even the very pebbles on the beach, rocks and mountains feel and sense emotions and human presence such that, whenever you interfere with them, they know so and feel it.

The idea of plants feeling pain is not a 'daft' one and is, in fact, true at times, for when you 'trim' them, do you not cut off part of them? They may not feel pain as humans do but they still feel this butchery, for that is what it is when done cold like the murder prepared in advance and then sprung upon the chosen victim. Plants, however, do not feel this fear for their mortal life because nature prepares for abundance and new life will always spring to the empty space. However, preparation is the key with all sentient creations. You need not ask their permission, but rather ask for their blessings and explain your desire to curb their growth. You may do this with your spoken words or your mind, but always with love and reverence for the perfect creation you have in front of you.

Do not fear, as you inflict no pain as a human would experience it, but your actions still cause upset and disorder in the natural way of things. Such is one of the ways humans inflict themselves on nature; respect it all, revel in its beauty and commune with your plants and animals, for they will intend your meaning and intentions whether they be good or bad. So too are the feelings of humans involved, affected and changed, for are we all not one? How can you be one with creation and not be affected, nay, changed, when you destroy a part of it?

So be it, scribe, we have many topics and questions to discuss. For your garden, send it love and commune with it daily in love, gratitude and adoration for all the beauty it so willingly, nay, lovingly, offers you and all who would just gaze and be one with its beauty. You cut not a plant as you would a fellow human, so be done with this idea and replace it with love and gratitude for all that plant offers you in its simple beauty.

For today we have finished the discourse on plants in your garden. Be done with this worry, this idea, for it serves you not. Be done with your idea of perfection too, for your garden or space will grow and blossom in its own perfection.

What about 'weeds' and brambles or other plants that would take over our gardens if not stopped?

Are they all not perfect in their creation? Commune with plants that would have their say in how your garden looks, for some are strong and would have their way in all your space, but never with the intention of causing you harm or with other malice. Command that these plants move back, or away, so that they cause no harm to any sentient beings — you or others. But regard all plants, trees and shrubs as marvels of creation, for that is what they are. Commune with your plants and command they grow not to their full abundance, but to your desired plan. And never wish harm on them or any others, for all will feel it. This sentiment of hate will echo through space and circle the world to join with other such sentiments to travel in a wave, nay, an ever-increasing tsunami, of violence and hate. As all such emotions do, whether good or bad, love or hate.

Be done with this topic now for we have discussed it at length and you tire of the topic. Rest now, scribe, till the morrow. Today you have written some important ideas and knowledge for others to understand and better know the land and world they, we, all live in.

Till the morrow, peace and love be yours, ours, today and evermore. Till the morrow, dearest scribe. Rest, remember and read this all with an open heart and without fear. Peace and blessings be yours, ours, today, and evermore shall it be so.

....

Friday, 24 April 2020

....

Dearest Yahvay, good morning to you on this beautiful day. Today I would like to ask you about gems and appreciating their natural beauty when mining causes damage to the environment. Is it 'wrong' to love gems? And do gems find or choose their owner?

Dearest scribe, good morning to you. Today your question is long with different facets to it. Gemstones are indeed wondrous creations of Mother Nature that have been loved and appreciated for millennia. However, as you rightly say, their mining, discovery and working do indeed destroy the setting they are found in. Digging, dynamiting and mining all cause damage to the land where the work is taking place. In all things, there is a balance, a deal to be done if you will. Whilst some mine responsibly with respect for the people and land where they work, others are less scrupulous and would tear down all to find the jewels they desire. Respect in all things is key. There is no 'wrongness' in loving, nay, adoring the beauty and bounty of what nature offers. This is not 'wrong', not an act that leads to harm others. The 'wrongness', if any, lies with those who would tear up the land in their frenzied search for the lucrative find. Respect is necessary, as are gentleness and an awareness of what such searches and mining result in.

Destroying a land filled with gems, or the odd gem, is not the best or most responsible way of doing things. For who can claim to have sovereign right over and under the land to perform such acts? Machines and modern ways will soon destroy any land if that is the will of those who drive such operations forward. To take and enjoy the bounty of your Mother Earth is a divine right, bestowed on you all for the pleasure of it in your lives. And so, there are many who love and would covet these glorious creations for themselves with the beauty and prestige the natural gems bring. However, there are also many who would bring harm to the land and the people who toil in these operations and mines. Here there is no respect for either nature or people. There are those who would dig and mine to leave their spoils, their machinery — once finished — to scar the land on the surface and underneath in the bowels of the Earth. Such ways are disrespectful and not in harmony with the balance of it all.

To love and adore the gems, these wonders of creation, is not 'wrong', how could it be so? But to love these wonders of creation and see them only for the value they bring in money, is not the way of those who are responsible and would steward the lands and Earth for all to enjoy, including nature and animals. So much harm can be inflicted on the innocent land in the name of success, in whatever form it takes. Mines and mining use much that is not in the natural way of things — and whilst this is not bad per se, for all things are offered to be enjoyed — the redress and restoration of the land are needed. Respect dictates these actions, and care is needed to ensure it happens and that all is restored to its natural state of beauty.

A love of gems is not 'wrong', for how could love ever be wrong? A love that entails cruelty to the land or people or animals is misplaced; unguided, unscrupulous. Ways that destroy or harm your home of planet Earth are to be renounced. Let a love, respect and gentleness pervade all actions, and let there always be respect for what is natural and beautiful, and for all those who would enjoy these things. Respect for all these things is also needed for yourself; would you consider buying from a thief? A pillager? Be honourable to yourself and shun those who would destroy your home in pursuit of their own riches and 'grandification'.

So be it, scribe. Beware those who would trick you and have you buy their sparkling trinkets, for they entail destruction to glitter on your finger. No gems have ever chosen to be wrought from the ground, nor even its destination onto your, or another's, finger. A gem will not call you, though there will be love forged between you and it, or them.

So be it, scribe. We have spoken at length again today. Rest now and consider what you have written and how it sits with you, your conscience and your pursuit of truth and what is fair and just in the world.

Rest now, for the day brings delights and the morrow brings more joy and words and wonders. So be it, gentle scribe. Go about your day in happiness for the joys it brings, and be satisfied with the words you have written today.

Till the morrow; in light, love and blessings as always, now and forever.

···

Sunday, 26 April 2020

···

Good morning, Yahvay, on this wonderful day. Today I would like to ask you more about gems and things of beauty. Why do we fall in love with certain things or find them beautiful, and not others? What causes this attraction?

Good morning, Lesley, dear scribe, you will find that you are quite overcome by the use, my use, of your name, something so personal on Earth and that rings the glory and sound of you and your spirit and 'journey' in this Earth lifetime.

Your question about beauty is really one on the value of beauty, for what a thing, a colour, a sparkle means to the beholder, the acquirent. Why do some things or gems sparkle to talk to us, our soul, in one way and other things not? Waves of love and joy and colour travel to us and through us in certain ways. The soul, your spirit, detects and feels these, and so either agrees to the feeling and energy or repels and rejects it. Such is the nature of beauty, especially gems and 'precious' items, on Earth. It's all an energy game. You find yourself, yourselves, in the midst of a giant energy field and grid. (*The image of a large, green mesh suspended around the Earth, though not touching it, forming connections between all of us, came to mind.*) Thus, certain things fit in with your position in this grid or they don't. Certain waves of energy sit well with you, whilst others don't.

The use of high energy, such as bombs, especially nuclear, disrupts this field and sends shock waves throughout the Universe. These shock waves affect you all and every sentient creation on planet Earth, and throughout the Universe. Such actions have untold consequences on you all; do not doubt these words or the truth they hold. For the consequences of certain human actions ripple back and forth through the Universe and time itself. Thus, actions of hate and violence today result in actions of violence and hate throughout time, including 'the past' and your past, your present life and present future life. It is all interconnected in the Grid, for it is a web so complex and all-encompassing that nothing cannot be in it and a part of it, even the tiniest molecule and its spaces all fall and fit into the pattern of the web, the Grid.

So it is that certain objects fit well into your space in the Grid while others don't. All sentient life fits into the Grid in its own space, but is at the same time connected with all other sentient, and seemingly non-sentient, creations. Your life, your feelings and actions, will all either be in harmony with the Grid or jar it, causing ripples in its form that ripple around or through the Earth and Universe. Thus, the actions of one represent the actions of all in the cause and effect they produce. Love calms all ripples and strengthens the bonds of the Grid, and the benefits are for all to feel and live in their daily lives. Acts of violence and hate hurt you all and disrupt the very essence of creation, its tranquillity and beauty, and above all its serenity and very way of being.

Thus, your things of beauty, your items of love, fit into your energy, your space in the Grid, or are for others, for the items to fit into their space and energy field. Though there is nothing 'wrong' or 'sinful' with desiring things of beauty, for they are an expression of your essence at a deeper level. But remember too, that living with less equates living with more, as an overload of items or things can suffocate or stifle the effects of the energy of love that the Grid has for all, and that travels to you all in your space in it. Thus acts, thoughts and feelings of love travel and strengthen the Grid for all to feel and benefit from. Conversely, acts of violence and hate ripple the Grid and weaken it and weaken all, whether they feel these energies or not. Some illnesses that cannot be explained by Earth's science and studies are created and lived by those who feel and perceive these negative energies; they are like sponges that soak up these vile actions and creations and their resulting energies. Love, restraint and peaceful ways support you all and enable the flourishing of life and its associated health. Such is the nature of beauty, peace and love in the universal way of things.

Rest now, dearest scribe, Lesley, for you have written well and in words of truth on an important topic arising from your seemingly simple question. Till the morrow, dearest one, for we grow ever closer and commune ever better. Let light, love and gentle ways be yours, ours, from this day forth. So mote it be. Ripples of joy and happiness be yours, ours, and let them fill the Universe for that is right and beautiful. Rest now, dearest one.

···

Wednesday, 29 April 2020

···

Good morning to you, dearest Yahvay. Today I would like to ask you about animals, their understanding of the world and life, and their feelings towards humans. Do our pets love us as we understand love?

Good morning to you, dearest scribe. You write in purple today, a most regal colour. Your questions about animals are many and important, for the world of humans needs to understand the beauty and balance that animals provide for you.

Each animal or creation has its own soul and spirit, independent of its species. All animals understand the passing of time and days and know the length of their life span, their natural life span. Can humans really understand such a simple and accepting way of life, such as the one animals possess? They *(the animals)* have no desire to better themselves or out-do each other; there may be a battle for supremacy, the lead role, but that is it. In their day-to-day lives, animals accept that there is a hierarchy and know their place in it, they accept this as the way of things and their lives. Animals do not attempt to vilify the Earth and other inhabitants. They take what is theirs and what they need, they have no greed for ever more. Humans would do well to adopt this simple philosophy and realise and understand that this simplicity works well.

An animal, like humans, is not born with a capacity to fear. This is a learnt emotion that serves animals well when there is a need to share, co-habit, the same space on Earth. Most animals fear humans as they see them as natural predators. Only the strongest of animals, or the bravest, would tackle a human. Though animals may seem unruly and unruled, there is a system to their organisation and groups, for they understand at a deep level the need for order and beneficial grouping; that is, groups or herds of the right number with the right order of things. In their natural state, animal numbers will grow to the maximum of the land. Once this number is reached, either migration is needed or death ensues.

Animals do not love each other as humans perceive love, but they do love others and, at times, humans. Thus, your pets, yes, they have so much love for you and a love that is purer than most people can understand. This love has shades of dependency as many animals are kept and housed in a place that is not their natural habitat. All animals respond with love to kindness, love and attention. Animals that are not regarded or respected can react with violence or anger. Thus, animals, too, have a spectrum of emotions that humans, in their limited capacity of spiritual being, can understand.

The soul of an animal is sacred, just as the soul of a human is sacred, for are they not all part of the same wondrous creation? Humans would do well to learn from the animal kingdom and world, for there is much they could study and learn from their 'fellow' spirits on Earth. Is not each creation a wonder to behold? So divinely created for its own part in the world on Earth?

Animals too suffer and fret and fear. They have learnt fear of humans from the violent and often destructive ways of people; from the cruelty and violence inflicted on them for the pursuit of pleasure — the pleasure of inflicting pain — or in the name of knowledge, of science, of 'learning'. Such are the ways of the calculating humans who see the Earth, its animals and flora as their playground, their 'scientific' laboratory. But this is not the way of things in the natural world, the animal world that is often filled with values and respect for all that would share their natural space, other co-habitants. From the iciest frozen tips of planet Earth to the hottest, most barren of deserts, you will find animals that can survive there as they understand and feel the energy of where they live. Humans have now sadly lost this ability, and as such always live in a barrenness that they themselves have created, pushing nature and its wondrous animals to the fringes of this barrenness.

Where there is green and peace or space to wander, a natural place, animals can, and will, survive and contentedly go about their ways. Where there is conflict, dispute over an area, animals fear and fret and fight to regain what was theirs. Humans have displaced and dislodged many animals and their habitats, for human numbers and greed for more ever increase. Thus, the plight and destruction of animals is widespread and takes on more than the natural way of things, the natural balance of things. Animals, too, have a wondrous place in the order of things, at times more wondrous and beautiful than that of their fellow humans.

Stop, scribe, for you tire of the topic and the writing. We have discussed at length what needs to be said on the animal kingdom today, but we will say more in the morrow for animals are a vital part of the holy creation on planet Earth, and the balance needed to respect all living things on this wondrous blue gem of the Universe.

Rest now and ponder on these words for you feel they have not satisfied your quest for better understanding when they have. Read with an open heart, and a better understanding of the way of things will be yours, ours, for we have asked and answered an important question with regard to all sacred life on planet Earth, your planet and home in this fleeting lifetime. Ponder on the truth of what you have written in the search for love and a better understanding of the way of things on planet Earth, and your human experience of life here, for it is but a fleeting moment and one that will soon pass in all its glory and triumph of being 'Scribe to the Universe'.

Dearest scribe, you tire; rest and be refreshed for the morrow when we speak further on the plight and blight of your animal friends and their ways here on planet Earth. Till the morrow, dearest scribe, Lesley. Let your name ring through the Universe and its sounds be written in the Book of Time, and in all secrets foretold and blessed from the moment of their creation forth. Be sure that it is so and rest, refresh and nourish your body and soul, and let these words make sense in your heart and the hearts of others who would, or would not, hurt their fellow co-habitants on planet Earth.

Enjoy your precious moments of miracles here on planet Earth.

Stillness and wonder be yours, ours, this day forth. So be it.

....
Thursday, 30 April 2020
....

Good afternoon, dearest Yahvay, another glorious day here. Is it now the morrow so we can continue our discussion on animals? And I would like to ask, if animals kill other animals or people, does this act affect the Grid of energy that we're all part of?

My dearest scribe, Lesley. You think long and hard about what you want to write and this is good for the words are for you, your delight and pleasure — as they are for others — and your learning, your grand study and yearning to understand all that is 'good', 'bad' and indifferent in the life that you lead on Earth. So be it. Our 'discussion' on animals will do well today for you are less tired and have a clearer mind.

When animals kill there is a purpose to their action, the purpose of living. When a human kills it is often with a grand desire to hurt, inflict injury; a lust for vengeance is often the reason the pistol trigger is pulled. An animal, however, on the other hand, does not keep a tally of rights and wrongs, of actions perceived as good or bad. An animal kills in order to survive or feed its young, or to be head of its pack or group. People have many emotions that they express in different ways, and sadly, murder and killing are just some of those expressions of an all-consuming anger or hate. Therein lies the difference and the key. Killing to live and for food differ greatly from killing to satisfy a vengeful lust, an all-consuming desire to kill, maim or destroy for the simple pleasure and gratification of doing so. Thus, the impact, the wave of energy created by either action is different in oh so many ways. A tsunami bathes the shores of its victims in a rush, a violent all pursuing rush of energy that gorges itself in the destruction it creates. So too is the tsunami of energy created by war and wanton destruction by humans, disrespectful of the land, of their home or the home of others.

Animals, in contrast, drop no bombs, do not hunt other animals to extinction and do not reduce their forest habitats to bare earth in the name of progress or equality or defence or in the name of any noble pursuit that is non-other than a desire to kill or destroy or create more money. As such, these intentions and all empowering energies are the ones that jar and mar the Grid, the flow of the Earth's energy, and the energy for all who live on and share this beautiful gem of a planet, Earth.

Such is the major difference on planet Earth, for intentions create actions and actions create results that all may feel or may benefit from. Such is the way of things on planet Earth.

So be it. And now for your next question that you have pondered on for many a day now.

Logically, as I see and understand it, if we are all one, then aren't you also part of the destruction of planet Earth and all the 'horrible' things that people do to others and animals?

Your question is an important one and needed to be asked, for if I am The Creator of all, then I must be The Creator of all that is good and bountiful, and also all that is bad and destructive. Your logic is right and I thank you for your thoughts.

In the far reaches of the vast and cavernous Universe lie and reside all emotions, just as on Earth and more, much more. A full spectrum of emotions is the human prerogative, the divine right to express and be all, good or bad. So too do I express myself through all these emotions and am like the sides, the multi-sides of any coin you may choose or imagine.

So yes, as for the destruction of your planet, am I not also involved? Do I not perceive the lust for money, greed, anger and frustration? The difference lies in my, our, choice of actions from thoughts of harm and decimation to thoughts of love and respect for others and our home of planet Earth. Would I decimate my own creation of planet Earth, the beautiful blue gem of the Universe, in a pique of rage? As the child would destroy its own toys whilst consumed in an all-embracing rage? Am I the child in a tantrum, as many would act and convey themselves, or the loving parent patiently waiting for that side of the coin to flip? For the anger to wane? May I not know these emotions and blindly follow their lead? Would I pursue such a lead? Such an action? Can love truly destroy the object of its desire? That I may experience these emotions, yes. That I may act upon them, no. For how could love, pure love, want anything other than love, peace, and blessings for all regardless of whether the object or person be 'good' or 'bad'? How could such a way be and exist in the name of love? And a love so deep for all that has been created on this beautiful, bountiful planet you call home; a speck in the Universe that is a part of me, my essence and my creation. So too is the duality of creation, that the very creation created may yet destroy itself and its creation. Such are the ways of the Universe.

The divine gift of choice is ever yours, ours. Your actions and thoughts, though guided by me and angels, result in your own thoughts and emotions, or the blockage of them. Many are blinkered and complacent that all is well and will ever be so, for they feel not deep in their hearts that they are divine creations, all-powerful creations created in the name of, and by, God. They have forgotten their true glory and the honest ways of true love. So, I am part of you all and part of the destruction too, for how could it be otherwise? But do I destroy in the name of love and greed and 'self-grandification'? No. Do I guide and urge you to do otherwise? Yes. Such is the contradiction of life on planet Earth. To have and to hold, to love and cherish, to be forever eternal is the true nature of love and all that is. To have and destroy, to hate and loathe, to kill in blood lust are perversions of the intrinsic nature of the Universe. No god or angel or any other part of the Universe would wish ill on any other part of the Universe or any other creation. Such a folly is a falsehood promoted by many, but baseless in the original glorious truth of creation and its expression of love. Can I be one and not the other? No, for there are always two sides to the coin — at least. Can I be one and not express the other? Yes, for I can be love, and feel and understand the emotion of anger or hate. Is it to be acted on? Not in the Universal way of things with love as its very essence and way of being. Emotions are there to be felt and understood, but not always acted on. Such is the nature of choice in the human world and life. To feel, understand and then act are all divine expressions of love and the divine gift of choice in all things, including your emotions. Act on thoughts of love, and express who you, we, truly are. Such is the light of love and all it brings to fruition. The divine choice is eternally yours, ours, as are the fruits of your, our, actions. Make the choice wisely and with consideration for all, including yourself, and always, but always, in the name of love and goodness for all.

So be it, scribe, for we have spoken at length on two important topics. The knowledge from your questions is important and knowledge that all will need to know to live their lives in glorious integrity and, above all, love.

Go about your day in peace and joy and know that you have written well and with words that will soothe the souls of many.

Peace and blessings be yours, ours, today and forevermore. In peace and love, dearest scribe, till the morrow.

MAY

And so, May is already with us! I can't believe it; we'll soon be halfway through the year! Where did those first months go?

Spring did not bring its usual showers in April. Perhaps they're here now to make up for the lost days last month. The days are still getting longer and the nights shorter, which is always so welcome after winter with its cold and dark.

Coronavirus is still with us all, in the UK, Europe, and the rest of the world. At last, there are some hopeful signs of the illness abating and not spreading so fast. At the time of writing (start of May), we are still in lockdown, as is most of the world.

I'm spending more time scribing and typing, whilst still managing to do most of the other things I would normally have done. I love being in contact with Yahvay regularly, and often wake up early to get going!

Happily, both my writing and typing are getting better, which is good, as the messages are getting longer. I'll finish my second notebook this month, and there's still lots more to scribe. My sleep is still much better than it has been for years, and I often wake up feeling refreshed, which is another new thing for me.

There are some strange things happening too. My favourite pencil has blocked and jammed so I can't use it! And another lovely pencil is now unusable, and a third one just disappeared. A thorough search of the house for more has revealed few, so I'll have to get some new ones. Now three of my watches have stopped — is this an omen of different times ahead? They aren't expensive, I just like to change my watch to go with my clothes, but it is nice to have a watch that works and tells the time. The garden people haven't been either, just to do the lawn, and that's the third week now. That's three lots of threes. How strange!

It's 22nd of May and the wind is very strong — nothing unusual there — but what is unusual is how dirty the air is and how much sooty dirt is being blown into the house. It makes me wonder how people in other parts of the world live if they have no windows they can close or water to clean all the surfaces; and how do people in refugee camps manage or those who live in arid parts of Africa?

. . . .

Friday, 1 May 2020

. . . .

Dearest Yahvay, good morning to you on this wonderful day. Today, could you tell me how you think? As a human, I use a physical brain (I think) to think. If you are spirit or pure energy, how do you think?

Dearest scribe, good morning to you and all those who read and ponder on these words, their truth and meanings. Thinking is a human function of a human life on planet Earth. To think is a physical activity that requires time, effort, and thought. The world of spirit does not need all these steps, for the knowledge and knowing are there for us to perceive, and is realised in stages. I created all knowledge and knowing, and as such, do not need to think or ponder, for I create both the question and the answer, as is written in the Book of Time — my book and me. I am the one who guides you through each day and whispers your thoughts of love into your heart. I do not need to think or ponder because the answer, the knowing, is already there, for I am the question and answer in one.

I am the essence of all things; I am in all things and cannot not be found. The questions and answers were deemed and written in eons past into The Book of Time and All Knowledge, for there is no question that I am not, and so no answer that I am not. In human life, you think, ponder and deliberate all possible outcomes to your question when the answer is always me and mine and yours to share in your experience of being human in life on planet Earth. Therefore, no knowledge cannot not be mine or me, for I am the knowledge, the font of all-knowing. I think not as you do, for I know the answer, as you already do deep in your heart. Thinking is a human activity, knowing is a spirit activity; a way of being for the world unseen and untold in your days on planet Earth.

I created all knowledge, knowing and truths according to the ways of love and me, my ways. For there is no other way than the way of love and all-knowing. Such is the way of 'reason' and 'thinking'. The brain would rule all and make you crazy or ill in its efforts to guide you along your road or path. Your heart speaks to me and knows the rights and wrongs, the best and worst of any question, for there is a knowing that requires no thinking, only feelings. Feelings of what is 'right' and 'good' and what is 'wrong' and serves you not. Thinking is human, knowing is divine and the right and way of the divine and the gods.

But who created the knowing, and how?

In the eons of the darkness and past in the Universe, there was only the whisper, the tiniest whisper of love in a vastness so vast that it is beyond the human capacity to understand or even imagine. That tiny whisper of light and love was me in my own creation of the Universe. I am the right and wrong of all, I am the space and fullness of everything you see, I am the pictures in your imagination, I am the way, and I know of all things now and forever. There is nothing I cannot be or feel, for I am the essence of all and in all things am I. I need no reasoning to understand and create the ways of the Universe, for I am the Universe and all things have I foretold and created. All things. When I know what your heart struggles with, I know the solution, the salve, the balm that would soothe it and comfort you in your human days and ways. Therefore, I think not as you do, I know as you do not. In all ways and all things is there a way, an answer, the revealing of light and truth — the revealing of me. Your prerogative and gift is choice and the ability to choose what suits you best as you believe your values and loves to be on planet Earth. So be it. You choose, and I know, you choose and I know. This simplicity is the truth of the Universe and all divine creation in the Realm of Spirit, the unseen world from planet Earth. So be it, scribe. We have discussed at length your question, an important one and one that needed to be asked. Rest now, for I know the day presses on you. Go about your day in love, peace and joy, and hold your head high with the honour of your mantle of 'Scribe to the Universe'.

So be it, gentle scribe, till the morrow. Peace, love and blessings be yours, ours, on this wondrous day and all the days to come in your life on planet Earth. So be it. In love, as always, Yahvay.

Dearest Yahvay, I have been thinking about your earlier comment on being the question and the answer. According to that idea, are all these questions yours, and none mine? Is that so?

Dearest scribe, you are right to ask this question for many will ask the same. Your role is 'scribe' and so I ask the question for you to scribe — or write — and then answer the very same question. Thus, your role, seemingly initially a small one, is, in fact, one of the grandest of all times, as is the role of other scribes who commune with the divine. These great writers, you included, perform a task beyond their simple human one, for few have the ability or patience to commune with the Divine as we do. Be not sorry or sorrowful that it is so, for our accord was thus eons past, while the glory and triumph of it all is written, nay, etched, into your future, 'Scribe to the Universe'. Few take on this mantle as few would try, and even fewer would have the responsibility of writing these sacred words. A human feat indeed, and worthy of recognition on planet Earth.

Rest now, for now you know the answer to our question, your question, my question — our question. Your mantle is special; wear it with pride for you hear or feel both the question and answer well. Henceforth I shall refer to our question if you prefer. The will and way and choice are ever yours; choose with love as your, our, guide. So be it, gentle scribe. We have spoken at length today on diverse topics. The morrow will bring us further delights and questions — yours or mine is unimportant compared to the importance, nature and topic of the question asked.

So be it, gentle scribe, till the morrow, for the day's task of scribing is now complete. Be pleased and happy with all that you do today. And rest and be sure that all is well and all is so in truth and love, as always, Yahvay.

Good morning to you, dearest Yahvay, on another wonderful day on planet Earth. Please tell me about my health changes that appeared after an accident.

Good morning to you, dearest scribe, Lesley. Today you ask a very personal question and one which many will be pleased you shared, as physical ailments in the frail human body can have many causes, some of which science and measurements and studies can't explain. There are many illnesses that fall into this category. Your health changes are personal to you, like unwelcome visitors that have taken up residence. Did you invite them into your life? In a way, yes, for many are the conditions in life that open the door to illnesses and malaises. This life has brought you sorrow and a sadness so deep that few would fathom it. Suffice it to say that your guests will soon leave, completely without a trace of them ever being there.

There are times when lives seem to clash, a person's lives throughout all time – now and forthwith *(the future)*. These clashes, when the lives sit not well together, can cause a jarring where the energies would overlap seamlessly and thus are not smooth or consistent, resulting in disfigurements of the energy where the different time energies meet. The results can be sudden and varied, but not always a serious condition.

In your case, the changes arise from the depth of your being, your heart, as it would express itself more deeply in your life, for you, and all that you do in your daily tasks. Your heart is bound by the chains of sadness and weighed down by fear for your life and future. *(Although this was a minor accident, I felt shocked afterwards and lost a lot of my confidence generally.)* These changes are like the desire for rebirth and renewal — a new stage or step in your life where you are the sole star and protagonist. Patience and self-love are the keys in this, as in many other cases. Adore the creation that you are, all of you, the mighty pillar arising day by day. Be still and fill your heart with happiness and joy, and feel it fill and swell with these emotions to the point where it breaks its bonds, its chains, and replaces fear with a newfound audacity. Such is the power of joy and happiness working with your mind and imagination for your good and robust health. Let your heart feel your joy and take part in the celebration of your life and no one else's. For there are days of heaviness and sadness caused by the love for another, your soul sister. Be happy and sure that all will adjust with time to the greatest of days and times.

For now, be content in all that you do and let your heart feel your newfound joy. For many ailments are subdued by joy, many are the unwelcome guests invited to leave by laughter, smiles and joy. Other ailments require a more personal understanding, as lives and emotions and energies are all variant in the milliards of souls and energies and lives throughout time on planet Earth.

Love, acceptance and understanding are always the keys to unlocking the door to the next chapter of your life.

So be it, scribe. Rest now for you have many more questions and answers to write on the great wonders of life and the Universe. In love, peace and blessings, as always, Yahvay.

Are there other illnesses or conditions caused by a sad and/or fearful heart?

You are right to ask, as many will wonder the same themselves. Fear and sadness felt in the heart can result in many conditions, such as psoriasis, arthritis — rheumatoid or other — gout, bloating, heart palpitations and Arrhythmia, fluid retention, heart attack and heart problems. *(Please remember, illnesses are personal. Follow any medical advice you may have been given.)* Many are the cases of 'strange' illnesses that cannot be explained by 'conventional medicine', that have their roots in an imbalance of energies, such as previously explained, and blockages of energies when there is trauma or strong emotions such as anger, sadness or guilt — guilt being a major player in the field of disruption. The mind and imagination can either work in your favour, or against you, causing blockages and problems programmed into the body through your imagination or repetitive thoughts and words that do not support you.

Each human body in its own space in the Grid is subjected to the energies of that person, the people close to them, and the people far from them but close due to the effects of the Grid. The situation is complex and unique to each person. As all the energies come to bear on a person they can, and will, be altered by the person's emotions, feelings, desires and wishes and beliefs. Each part has a role to play in the state of health of each person, and each person affects the health of those close by, and those far away, by affecting the Grid.

The coronavirus illustrates how health, your health, can be affected by someone half a globe away, on the other side of planet Earth. Though we speak of a virus that has claimed many lives, its power and presence are multifold in its efficacy. Fear gives any illness strength and the wings it needs to travel further in your own body or touch the health of others. Fear and all negative emotions provide the horse for an illness to trot or gallop ever faster. Fear too, can travel the distance of the Earth and claim many victims in its path.

Righteousness, self-belief and love can negate fear and halt it in its progress; for once it takes hold, fear can, and will, take you to dizzying heights only to drop you broken at the time it desires. So too are the emotions of anger and hate; they too will carry you along their path, their destructive path, only to leave you alone in your desolation and fury in a blind, dark alley. No person should pursue these emotions or let them take hold in their life, for unbridled they will take you where they will (want to). Outwardly nothing much may seem different, but inwardly these feelings and emotions can, and will, take up residence in your body. Once there and stable, settled, they can, and will, grow if left untended so that they interfere with the natural balance of things in the delicate human body you all reside in.

Your body speaks to you in messages of pain, of malaises, of ailments, when its natural, beautiful balance is affected or threatened. Heed your body's words, tend to it and lavish it with love and laughter — the best soothes and 'medicine' you can offer it. Be your own light and joy, every day, and heed not others who would make you sad or angry. Their emotions can, and will, put you and others out of balance. It is all one Earthly picture, with the specks of people all affecting themselves and each other. So, in all things let love, joy and gentleness be your ways for yourself and those near you and those far away in Earth terms. For in reality all life and distance are here and now. Mark these words well and live their truth today and forever.

Rest now, dearest scribe, the day and its needs press on you. So be it. We will commune further on this topic.

....
Monday, 4 May 2020
....

Good morning to you, dearest Yahvay, what a wonderful day it is! What shall we talk about today? Shall we continue the topic of health?

Good morning to you, dearest scribe, Lesley. For now, we have discussed at length the topic of health. You have other questions you would ask. Please do so, ask our next question.

Please tell me about the role of parenting. Is it true we choose our parents before we are born?

Your question relates to a topic that is discussed much and at length on planet Earth. The role of a parent is the role of guardian and teacher in one. Your parents are in fact chosen before your human birth, decided, arranged and agreed in the Realm of Spirit where all knowledge pervades and resides. There are lessons to learn on planet Earth, that playground of life for humans to enjoy and learn in. The rough and tumble of life there, here, is one of the most sophisticated in terms of lessons learnt and values understood. Learning can take place on the whole of the planet, for all to understand, and in ever-smaller units of country, region, family and the individual whose learning is wide-fold in all these variables and conditions. Thus, any member of any family can, or will, be influenced by the roles of the parents and the lessons they offer. They too *(the parents)* are in turn influenced by others they meet, their own parents, and this line can go way back into the distant 'past' — for remember, time is an illusion and in reality all time is now — all the people they meet and deal with, their region and country.

Mass movements and ideas may sweep the globe, updating knowledge and understanding or depleting it to move onto a new era of philosophy and values and ways of looking at the world: a global understanding. This global understanding can now take place at an ever-increasing speed and accuracy at times, for your, our, human technology allows and enables this. However, whilst these advances are many and enable or aid many, they take away from you and your natural ways of being, and understandings of your essential nature, your natural essence and skills and abilities.

The role of technology pervades all lives to some degree, and now we see how it too becomes a parent. For the screen and its images preside and dominate in many houses and young lives, thus, the role of parenting at present is diminished and handed over to a monstrosity *(this seems a strong word, but no other word came to mind)* of a box where alien thoughts and ideas, values and ways are passed onto the innocent mind of a child. This was foreseen in the Book of Time in all its revelations, for it was programmed thus that people would turn increasingly to an artificial means of entertainment and the dispersion and uptake of other people's ideas. This network of knowledge favours the few in its creation but influences the masses in its effects, and results in a diluting of the family units, a slackening of the family ties. Whether this is 'good' or 'bad' for the individual depends on the quality of the information and the way such information is received and perceived.

In reality, the guiding hand of a loving parent is always needed to ensure that the first steps of the baby into its life are the right ones for the path it has chosen. In the world today, on planet Earth, many steps are now taken and many lessons learnt with the added parent of technology in the form of a phone, computer or television. This way was foretold as it is a lesson, a global one, for all to see and understand the ways of creation that are not natural and so do not satisfy or nurture the soul of many as would the natural ways, ones of beauty, peace and tranquillity; the ways of creating and being one with nature and the Realm of Spirit and all natural energies.

Thus, parents too are disempowered by the advent and continued use of technology, which whilst advantageous, also has its detractions. Thus, the role of parenting and the lessons it offers is now shared, not with other parents or family members as in generations past, but with strangers, unknowns, who have their own agendas, views and beliefs on life. This trust can be misplaced but is often not questioned for this is the 'modern' way of things and of life on planet Earth in its present phase. This too will change as a new wave of ideas, a different philosophy of life, will sweep the Earth and replace these ideas with new ones, some may say 'better' ones. The present virus is part of the resetting on planet Earth and the values that have pervaded the world up till now. This resetting will touch all and never again will their values return to the previous ones 100%. Thus, the role of parenting is now in a state of flux and many will be the parents who relish, and would return to, the days of abandon of their offspring, to re-delegate the responsibility of being a 'good' parent to the schools, teachers and technology. 'Modern' ways with 'modern' outcomes, the results of which are paid every day by those in society who dig into their pockets to repair the 'damage' of such abandonment, and wonder why and how things have come to this outcome, when they themselves have played a part in its creation — as you all have. The present times in the days of the virus will teach you all different things and leave different memories and resources in its path.

Your ways of schooling and education do little to improve young minds beyond the learning of random, mandatory facts, ways and information designed to perpetuate the ways of your present societies. Young minds cannot, therefore, cultivate their natural skills and abilities as schools and schooling have little or no room for such strengths and benefits to the individual and society; a society that must always be regulated to maintain its artificial ways and norms. That is the way and wonder of your 'modern' world and all its success. Build the towers ever higher so that all may fall ever further and lower.

Parents too are engulfed and engrossed in this myriad of rules and ways. Their input is ever less and ever less influential and informative, such are the ways and wonders of your 'modern' life and world. Where parents influence and control their children less, there is more room for spontaneity, whether this be 'good' or 'bad'. Thus, room is created for the young ones on planet Earth to explore all aspects of life without the constraints of tradition or established ways of doing things. The outcomes, or results, may vary from more independent thinking to more conformist thinking in that youngsters then fall into the established ways of expressing themselves through violence and violent acts. Parents now have an ever-weaker voice whilst the outside, with all its values, encroaches ever more into the family life, values and ways of doing things. Such is the plight and blight of the 'modern' world and its inherent values. Generations are being lost to the 'new' order of things and all the 'wonders' this may hold. Such is the 'modern' playground of life on planet Earth.

Tuesday, 5 May 2020

Good morning, dearest Yahvay, another beautiful day here. Please tell me more about the changes and resetting of the world that you referred to yesterday.

Good morning to you, dearest scribe, Lesley. You have started your day well with acts of love for others and gratitude, two essential acts in human life on planet Earth, and I thank you for these.

The great resetting and resultant changes that are happening now on planet Earth were programmed and foretold in the 'Book of Time' eons ago. The present resetting will feel brutal and harsh to many, especially those who lose loved ones to the Realm of Spirit. Such is the way of things when great changes happen and take place, wherever or whenever they may be. The present virus will sweep the Earth several times in its wave of change and resetting. Many of the old ways will fall to one side in the wake and consequent resetting of your human lives and ways. When all is cleared, the bodies buried and the silence broken, there will be a global questioning of the cause, the reason for it all, before the frantic rush to return to the all-consuming monetary ways recommences.

But there will also be a stillness, a reticence to resume things and life as they were prior to the wave of change swept in by the coronavirus. Many will be the sick who recovered, and even more the number who found peace and tranquillity during the grip of the illness. Their voices will be heard and felt around the world on planet Earth — voices that would not return to the politic and monetary satisfaction of an ever-increasingly fast-paced life. It is now time to stop, slow down, and smell the daisies along the side of the road. So much of so many lives has been lived in haste and pressure and fear and isolation, for you only have to look at your ever-mounting bills and wonder why this 'glittering' lifestyle sits not well with you, for the sparkle soon fades and the next glitter must be bought or achieved. You find the caged hamster running ever faster on its wheel amusing and realise not that you are all like the hamster — caged and trapped to run ever faster without making any progress or change, and living a life that is empty and devoid of true, deep satisfaction. Think of this hamster, this beautiful creation, and consider the life you would have it lead. For how can a cage with basic comforts truly represent life, a free life, and honour the basic skills and capabilities of that animal? Can it? Can it truly? Now consider the cage you have forged with your very own hands and volition, and ask how your lives are different, if at all. You may wonder at this simple analogy but keep it close to your heart, not your mind, to hear the whispers of truth said in love and with love for you. Your mind would have it otherwise and refuse such a comparison for it sees the value of all that glitters in your lives on planet Earth. But stop, be still and feel the truth of how your lives are alike and match in all senses of being and not being, which is the denial of your true selves and your true power and the glory of the eternal beings that you all are.

The next wave of consciousness to sweep the world will bear the traces of this awakening and realisation that the account books and numbers do little to take you all off your ever-spinning hamster wheel. 'There must be more' will be heard in the voices of many, the many who would have change and not return to the 'old' ways. Many are the voices that will be raised, and many will be the voices of 'reason', habit and tradition that would return to the old ways with which they are comfortable and understand. This voice of 'reasoning' now belongs to an era of past usage and 'success', for a life driven by balance sheets, numbers and money will always find a way to equate success, without figuring the true cost of the ways that lead to this 'success'.

The voices of rebuttal and refusal will grow in number to the point where your airs remain empty with little other than the wind and the air you would breathe, your roads and rails quieter for what good will they serve when technology allows for little or no movement to a workplace? Your factories will quieten and gorge out less, for less will be the incessant demand for ever more, ever more (*in the sense of time*). A stillness will pervade and a silence filled only with bird song will resume as the way forward. Silence, stillness and happiness found in being contented with less, will ever grow and fill your lives with a serenity not known greatly before the sweeping of the virus. This will be the next phase on planet Earth. An acceptance that there is a limitation to all things, especially those that would bring you joy. A denial and refusal of the next glittering triumph or trophy with an easiness, a willingness to let go and let be. This new way will creep into being, nay, slide into your ways in the stillness in the wake of the virus and its all-encompassing, sweeping wave of change. Take heart those who would have less to have more in terms of serenity and the satisfaction of just being, being alive here and now in the new era of epic change.

And so concludes our discussion on today's topic of change and the new ways that will sweep the world in the wake of the present, all-encompassing virus and viruses.

So be it, gentle scribe, Lesley. For the day we have done. Go about your day and life in peace and be pleased with all that you achieve this day as on all days. In peace, love and blessings today and always, Yahvay.

....
Wednesday, 6 May 2020
....

Good morning to you, dearest Yahvay, on this wonderful day. Please tell me about souls and spirit. Are they the same thing?

Good morning to you, dearest scribe, Lesley, for you have asked an important question. Souls and spirit are not the same, though many would use the words interchangeably. A soul resides in a person and is an essence in human incarnation. The soul is the essence of that person for that lifetime and beyond. But a soul is not restricted to one person or lifetime, and in fact will return many times to that playground of life on planet Earth to have human experiences in diverse lives and in both genders — either as a man or a woman. Your soul is the core of your being, it is who you are and will always be. In contrast, spirit refers to the energy of an unknown person or persons. It is the core of what they are, as opposed to, for example, matter or a solid object. Thus, your soul resides in your body and is the spirit part of you. Your soul leaves your body and remains your soul to live on in the Realm of Spirit. Therefore, the terms are not strictly interchangeable, as one refers to the essence and the other refers to its energy — its form if you will. Thus, when speaking of the spirit of a person we refer to the energy part of that person, or even the land or the flowers or the trees, you are talking about the energy that may be perceived and felt. The Earth too has a soul, an old soul that has been much maligned and disregarded over time and the history of humans. All souls are spirit in their formation, but not all spirit is the soul of an entity.

Some souls can remain trapped in their Earth experience and their spirit, or energy, can be seen or felt by those who are sensitive to such energies and open to the idea of such. A trapped soul is a soul often in need of help and assistance to re-join the Realm of Spirit. Such an undertaking should not be taken on lightly, for a soul in distress may wish you harm or wish to cause mischief. As in all things, love is the answer, and blessing a trapped soul will aid its progress and movement to the other side, the side of joy and eternal love.

So concludes our short topic for the day.

Rest, be in love and love all. Peace, blessings and joy to you today and forever, Yahvay.

Yahvay, did we finish the topic this morning?

Rest assured that we have finished the topic for now, we will return to it at a later date.

Yahvay, are you beginning to sound more like me?

We are one, dearest, and so with time our thoughts and ways will start to mingle and morph. Fret not, dearest one. Now you feel reassured. Go about the rest of your day with ease and lightness, and be content that you have written well on the topic for today.

Dearest Yahvay, good morning to you on this glorious day. If the world's population keeps increasing, are new souls created for all those new people?

Good morning to you, dearest scribe, Lesley. You struggle today and your thoughts come with difficulty, so be it. Our discussion on the number of increased souls will proceed well and in fullness, for your mind will clear with the writing.

New souls can be born at any moment and created in an instant, but that is not the way of things in the Realm of Spirit for we fill the Universe in love and with our energy. You think, or equate, one soul with one person, but that need not be the case for a soul may inhabit two or more bodies at the same time, at any given moment. Such is the growth of the spirit realm with its own unique ways of being that this is possible on an energetic level. Human bodies are confined to one space and place in the Grid, this does not apply to the Realm of Spirit where spirit can be in diverse or different places at once, at the same time. For in reality there is only here and now, no past or present, no here or there. The human brain often struggles with this concept as it only knows physical constraint to its being. This is, or may be, due to the physical laws present on planet Earth that conduce your life so. In the Realm of Spirit, these physical laws of planet Earth do not affect us and so we are able to fill the role of diverse souls in what, in Earth terms, is different times. And thus, different lives can be led by one soul in different bodies at seemingly different times and places.

There is no limit to the number of bodies a soul may inhabit, though this is not generally done as each soul would relish and enjoy to the full each human experience. Each body thus may have one soul living the different experiences that chosen life offers and was agreed on before the soul came to be born as a baby, as a child on planet Earth. Therefore, the number of souls does not need to increase in line with the ever-growing human population. Such is the way of things and how the Realm of Spirit knows all and can accommodate and plan for changes in the human world on planet Earth. Thus, concludes this topic for now, for we will discuss the Realm of Spirit further at a later date, another morrow if you will.

Now ask me 'your' next question, one you have pondered on for many a day now.

Please tell me about the importance of colour.

Colour is one of the most wondrous creations of the Universe, together with light. Can you imagine a world with no colour? What a drab, dark affair that would be. Colour and colours resonate with you at a very deep level for they touch your soul in different ways and thus resonate with the energies of your body, and as a consequence, the Grid in different ways. Thus, the importance of colour to you in your life cannot be overstated or undervalued. To live in colour is a basic need for you, your body, your mind and ultimately, your health.

Colours vibrate at different speeds as do the centres in your bodies designed to receive and store these vibrations. Thus, a world of grey, of concrete, is a flat world and leaves little benefit to those who live or reside there for any amount of time. Compare the harsh deadness of your concrete and tarmac with the vibrancy and wonder and life of Mother Nature and all that is natural and glorious in any natural setting. To be in nature restores you, your mind, your bodies and your energies, and any who would spend time thus will feel the benefits to their wellbeing. In contrast, as is often the way in your 'modern' world, those entrapped in the concrete wonders of a 'modern' city or town, will feel their energy deadened, depleted, for the body and thus, the soul, need colour and the vibrant energy of nature to flourish and thrive.

Colour comes to you all as a gift, it is the gift of living on planet Earth that stirs your heart and mind in the most subtle of ways. Thus, colour and light are as essential and basic as the air you breathe and would have at any cost. Light gives way to night, that moment of restoration whereas light gives invigoration in its brightness and splitting into colours for your joy and delight and benefit. Such is the role of colour, and one not to be underestimated. The different colours have different values for your body and mind and, as many of your studies have already shown, affect you and your mind; though in reality, it is your heart in different ways. Thus, colours speak to you, and your essence, in different ways for different reasons. A colour will 'shout' to draw your eye to it, for your body knows which colour it would have and why.

On Earth, there are colours associated with angels, but this need not be so for no angel needs one colour to perform or be efficacious in its deeds on planet Earth and throughout the Universe. Colours are also associated with energy points in the body and this is a good understanding, albeit simplistic, of one of the roles of colour and how it may serve you in your daily lives. Of all colours, the Realm of Spirit boasts the strongest, the most pervasive and invigorating and restorative, as spirit cannot, and would not, dull such a cacophony of visual delight as is the case on planet Earth.

Colour would sing to you in the wind, in the rain and in its rainbow if you would hear and understand the lyrics. Such a song is the breath of life for the 'blind', that is those who cannot see the true beauty of life on planet Earth. Colour would wash you of your 'sins' if it were the river of life, and would take you with it to the vastest of oceans in glorious 'technicolour'. The most vibrant of all colours is heartfelt, not mind felt, and would be breathed into your soul for that is where it may reside and flourish.

. . . .

Friday, 8 May 2020

. . . .

My dearest Yahvay, I feel your presence ever more and it brings me great happiness. I think I hear you, too, when I am not scribing, and

I really hope that that is the case. The last few days the writing has felt 'flat' after finishing it. Is that me or have things changed?

My dearest scribe, Lesley, the writing has indeed been flat and less of your usual sparkle. Thoughts and ideas can sit in your mind so quietly that you think they are not there and forget them, though their presence is known and noted and felt by your heart. For today let us continue our discourse on colour, as it was left unfinished and devoid of much meaning or sentiment to you. Suffice it to say that colour is an important topic for you and one felt close to your heart, as you love colour and shades, and the effects of light and dark and all the ensuing hues. You have an artist's eye and would secretly covet the idea of painting great creations in your medium of acrylic. Colour touches the hearts of many, especially those who work or play with its glory in the creation of their artistic endeavours created to the delight of many.

Colour ranges change with time and the setting. Thus, colours on planet Earth have different values and properties to colours in the Realm of Spirit where the very particles of colour may be perceived as light, and thus, colours possess and 'behave' in a different way. Colour in the Realm of Spirit is alive, almost a living entity in its vibrancy and energy, an energy that is unknown on planet Earth for your colour on Earth has little vibrancy, or level of energy, as in the Realm of Spirit.

So concludes our discourse on colour, for it is an energy that all would have, but few are the people who understand why, and the true benefits of this magical creation. Rainbows are the only light and colour creation to be truly felt by all those who witness such a spectacle and hold it dear for the magicness of it and its unheralded beauty. Such is the joy of colour that your heart, body and soul feel for this all-important creation. Use it at will, for the colour you need will present itself to you as beautiful and one that is needed in your life. Let this colour come into your homes, on your apparel or in your art and ornaments. Such are the joys of colour, especially in nature where the mastery of its use is unbridled and unparalleled in the human world of creation. Let colour speak to you all and weave its magic in your hearts and lives, and know that it would speak to you in tones and shades of love.

So be it, scribe. For today we have concluded our discourse on colour and its benefits. Go about your day in peace and love and feast upon the delights of the magic of colour.

So be it. Till the morrow, gentle scribe, Lesley. Let love, light, blessings and colour light and be your way. Till the morrow, dearest one, Yahvay.

Dearest Yahvay, I've been thinking, or maybe we've been thinking, can I command a cure for someone?

Dearest scribe, dearest Lesley, you can command that beneficial energies be and surround that person and fill the house for their benefit. You can command a miracle for their benefit if they would want one. Such are the ways of the Universe that only when a miracle is truly desired and heartfelt and believed, can it take place. Remove your blinkers as to what is possible; light your candle, be still and command that the Universe conspires with you to bring healing to all who dwell in the house. So be it.

· ·

Saturday, 9 May 2020

· ·

Good morning to you, dearest Yahvay, on another beautiful morning. Please tell me about time, as I don't fully understand it. You said time on Earth is an illusion, but often refer to the time in the Universe. Are they different? Is our way of measuring time the illusion?

Dearest scribe, your mind is full of the things you must do and organise. Fret not for it will all work out well and to your satisfaction. Your future too is on your mind, but fret not as the morrow beckons and is ever brighter with the joys of a newfound life and freedom.

Your question about time is, in reality, a question about the reality of all things, for all things sit together in a bond, or mesh, if you will. There are no different times, there is only one time that pervades all creation throughout the Universe and on planet Earth. The difference lies in how time is perceived, for it is fluid and static at the same 'time'. Therefore, your earthly time is governed in a false and mechanical way by the use of clocks and timepieces. In reality, all time is now, that is 'past', 'present' and 'future'. This idea sits not well with the human concept and will of dividing time into small units to be measured and studied and regarded with desire or regret. Therefore, there is no such division of time in the Universe, for all time is now and ever has been.

Time is not what it seems, as it can be manipulated for your benefit and delight. Your actions, thoughts and feelings today can, and will, alter your past, your now and your future as how you feel now is all of those. All your time is now and ever so. You think as a clock, always moving forward, or in one direction, without ever going anywhere or in any direction. For though the hands move, time does not, though the months change, and the days come and go, there is no difference in time itself — only the markers; your artificial markers on planet Earth that you would ever use to mark out and divide the illusion of time passing, when this is not the case at all.

And so, when you understand that all is now and ever-present, you are able to also see that your life, your actions, are in a bubble; one in the milliards of bubbles present on planet Earth. These bubbles may float and drift, but the essence inside is still you clambering to do all in your life while being suspended above it all in your bubble. The bubble is time that holds you in its palm, within its creation of the bubble, static while you rush and fret and try to achieve ever more; while in 'reality' your life and presence are suspended in inanimation, in a void if you will. Add to the bubble the essence of who you are today, who you were yesterday, a year ago, a lifetime ago and you will see that it is all suspended in a nothingness other than the fragile bubble that would hold it all. Your bubble with your life in it. Stand away from your bubble and observe how the tiny figure inside moves frantically to do all, to run and rush and complete its ever-growing demands of life. Stop and observe and consider the lunacy of passing your lives thus, and the falseness of your time divisions and marcations. All time, is now. The Universe is not filled with your bubbles – remember this was an analogy — for time flows seamlessly throughout it all. Time is but one facet of love and governs many aspects of the Universe in its own way, always with love at its core and its very essence. It is the almighty force that is ever-present, ever now and ever bonding, as time holds the Universe together in its grip, its hold. Love is the essence of the Universe cradled in the hold of time and its mighty force. Black holes escape the effects of time but are still held in its grip.

Your time, dearest, is an illusion that aids the governance of your days and life on planet Earth. In the Universe time has a much greater and powerful role to play as it is the bind that holds us all; like a cradle for a baby, it is there to hold, support and confine with its boundaries of love, force and power.

Thus, concludes the topic of time and its illusions — created by humans on planet Earth for their, your, our, convenience and understanding of life and lives on planet Earth. So be it, scribe. One of the greatest wonders of the Universe is time, a force so strong it holds all in its power — even your quill now is held by that force.

Rest now for you have scribed well and written much. In love, peace and blessings now and forever, Yahvay.

....
Sunday, 10 May 2020
....

Good morning, dearest Yahvay, on this wonderful day on planet Earth. Please tell me your thoughts on karma.

Good morning to you, dearest scribe, Lesley. You rose early this morning with the excitement and joy of writing, and your new pink keyboard. Such are the joys of life!

Karma is indeed an important topic, and one that has created much debate over the years. Suffice it to say that karma per se does not exist as there is no need for debts to be paid from one life to the next, a type of punishment if you will. Meting out a punishment would require a decision based on merit or 'badness', a consideration of the quality of a person's life. This, in turn, would entail judgement, which would entail deciding on, or deeming, an action or a life as 'good' or 'bad'. The Realm of Spirit and I don't use judgement as a way of being. Therefore, if a person has experienced and done 'bad' things, there will be a redress or a balancing, if you will, in the next life — perhaps. In any situation on planet Earth, there are always two options — the way of love and the way of not-love, in human terms and linguistics. So, any action, thought, or emotion will fall into the choice of love or not-love; it cannot be otherwise. Therefore, in some lives the results of actions of not-love will be perceived and acted on or received. Whether the receiver acts in love or not-love is unimportant as this will be the way, the plan of their life. The cause and effect, the acting on or receiving of love or not-love depend all on the grand plan, the designs if you will, of that person's or those persons' lives.

The picture is complex as often groups of souls will together decide on their preferred experiences for a human incarnation, and the life or lives they would lead. As a group, roles will be decided and agreed upon for the various and diverse experiences desired in a lifetime on planet Earth. Thus, a life of giving may be followed by a life of receiving — in whatever form of receiving this may be. For giving and receiving too, will fall into acts or actions of love or not-love. The choice is ever yours, ours.

Karma as a system does exist, but not in the way a human may perceive it. For it is known and noted all the acts of a person's life, but not with the intent of punishment or reward, but rather a difference of experiences; that is, either to receive or not receive love or not-love. The options are few, the outcomes and possible experiences infinite, almost as infinite as the Universe itself. Thus, a lifetime spent honouring not-love as its goal and way of being may be followed, at some point, by a lifetime of love as its essence and way of being. The choice is ever yours, ours, to experience the vastness of possibilities in the Universe, and all the lessons and experiences it may offer you.

Groups of souls may often incarnate together, but with differing roles as pre-decided in the Realm of Spirit. Thus, various, and oft-important experiences, can be lived together on planet Earth. The goal of the experiences will, of course, be to live and feel love or not-love in a lifetime, though these experiences may too change during the course, or courses, of a life or lives. To love or not love; to act in humility and grace or to act in boastful, bombastic not-love ways are your choice. Whether it be this lifetime or later, these actions and emotions will be carried out and lived, experienced.

Thus, karma as a system, its simplistic ways of retribution, does not exist in the Realm of Spirit, for no form of punishment could be, or ever will be, entertained or considered. Love is the preferred way of the Universe; love in all things and ways. So, a system designed on love or not-love that decides, nay, values, and deems a life as 'good' or 'bad' does not exist in the Realm of Spirit, but rather a way of being, of considering and valuing different experiences of a human life on planet Earth. Such is the way of all things, love or not-love.

There will be those who rant, nay, scream, at the seeming injustice of their lives on planet Earth; what other people have or have not done to them in their lives, for they feel the injustice of it all and their hearts weigh heavy. However, as in all things, there is a balance and experiences to be learned and lived. For how can you understand the true depth of love in all forms and ways without too experiencing not-love in all its ways and forms? Love and hate, which is not-love in reality, light and dark, 'good' and 'bad' are all two sides of the same coin; for how could you experience one and truly understand it without

115

experiencing the other? Would the light of day be as glorious if it did not follow the darkness of night? Would the smallest act of love not be understood, were it not for the acts of not-love experienced? Were there no duality, experiences of contrast, if you will, would have little or no value for the growth and understanding of the ways for a human soul. Thus, acts of not-love sweeten and brighten all acts of love. But remember that love is the true way of things, though there is always a balance and a choice — your choice, our choice.

Your soul group of fellow souls will too play their part in your life. Though you recognise them not is indifferent, for the experiences they offer are paramount as is your life and your role or roles in theirs. The balance is always struck, an accord reached for all souls to live, learn and experience together in their groups, of whatever size they may be.

Do not question 'why' in your life, as this serves you little, but rather 'what'. What is my experience? What are my feelings or emotions? What can I do to remedy this situation of not-love? Acceptance is key in many areas, but acts of love always, but always, bring joy to your heart in this life or another.

So be it, gentle scribe, for you have written well on an important topic and the discourse has been long but illuminating. Go about your day with the satisfaction of having scribed well on an important issue. I thank you for 'your' question — a very good one I might add.

In light, love and blessings to you and all you may meet this day forth, Yahvay.

· ·

Monday, 11 May 2020

· ·

Good morning to you, dearest Yahvay, on this wonderful day. Please tell me more about colour and how it's used in the body.

Good morning to you, dearest scribe, Lesley. 'Your' question today requires and necessitates the discourse of further details on the properties of colour and how it fits in with the energy centres in the body. Such centres have been rightly located in the body and given the name of 'chakras', a term that is now widely used.

Of all the colours, white and gold are the most essential. White, because it contains all the other colours, and gold for its colour of association with angels and divinity. All colours affect and aid your body in different ways. For example, your personal colour of joy is yellow, like sunshine. Whereas green aids your health, blue and purple are regal colours and also aid your connection to the divine, red is your colour of emotion and heat, whereas white and yellow are cooling colours for you. Each person is different in the respect of the colours they are drawn to and the benefits they hold for that person.

With regard to colour and the centres, for ease of purpose let's address them as chakras. These energy points in the body are like wells, and there are many more than the seven chakras oft cited, which absorb and then radiate the colours needed and used by your body. Colour has the function of aiding the completion of your body as an energy field, which is what the human body is in reality. It is but an energy field with various components — organs and bones for example. As an energy field in its natural state, the body is highly efficient and capable of great feats. Your modern life with its modern 'progress' has led to the compromise in the efficiency and well-being of this natural energy field. Microwaves, electricity, radio waves, television waves, telephone antennae, pollution and contaminated food — that is, food produced on a mass scale — all interfere with the natural balance of the energy in your bodies. Add to this the effects of stress, poor sleep, little rest or relaxation and the body is further compromised in its efficaciousness.

Imagine, if you will, a prism with its ability to split light or at least show the different colours of apparent white light. Now consider a rainbow with its beautiful arc of light in colours and the magic of it. So too are the colours of white light split when entering your body for its aid and succours. Your body is an energy field designed to function on planet Earth and use to its advantage these different colours of light that it lives in and is surrounded by. This is but one of the wonders of humans, created from the divine plan to sit in harmony with the world and life as it is naturally on planet Earth.

Colour can aid all bodies by flowing to the centres, or chakras, where it is needed. This flow, which indeed it is, seeps through the body to arrive at the centres in the different places in the body. All colour and colours are needed and used by the body, for all colours have different functions and benefits to you and your body and your mind. White is the universal colour in that it contains all other colours for your benefit. Thus, seeing yourself in white — apparel or light — brings healing and calming benefits to your body, mind and spirit, and energy field and make-up. Black, however, would drain your body of its vital energy and is thus oft associated with death in many parts of the world. Green, your heartfelt colour, is both a colour of love and healing, whereas orange is a vibrant colour which encourages the joys of life, sexual or otherwise. Purple, the most regal colour, is associated with royalty, thus power and this includes divine power too. Purple is a spiritual colour for those who would work or endeavour to make connections with this realm, the Realm of Spirit. Yellow is the colour of the sun, traditionally, and brings vitality with it into the body. Blue, a cool colour, is beneficial in calculated, careful communication and is especially beneficial where considered words are needed and careful thought formed. Red, a hot colour, is used as a warming colour in and by the body; it is for this that exposed blood is red as it shows the body losing its colour of warmth and thus, vitality.

All these colours, and more, enter the body and alter its energy to varying degrees. Thus, your apparel should reflect as wide a range as possible of all the colours, but preferably not black, which would drain the body of its energies. Colours are absorbed into the body through light, especially sunlight, and from the colours of your apparel. Once in the body, the energy field you reside in, colours will move to the centres or parts of the body where they are needed for the function of the body, its repair, and regulation and maintenance. Thus, a spectrum of light hitting the body will be absorbed in the individual rays of colour, which are then directed to the best place.

(I stopped here as the message did not feel strong or completely right.)

Yahvay, today has been a bit difficult and flat. Have I scribed all you wanted to say on the topic of colour? And accurately?

Fret not, dearest Lesley, for you have scribed all that is needed for the day. The morrow will bring the joy of a new topic and we can, and will, return to the topic of colour at a later date — another now if you will.

Rest now and be happy at what you have done today, for the book grows well in topics and volume.

Till the morrow, dearest scribe. Fare well. Love, light and blessings, Yahvay.

. . . .

Tuesday, 12 May 2020

. . . .

Good morning to you, dearest Yahvay. Another wonderful day here on planet Earth. Today, could you please tell me about my (accidental) fall last year?

(This fall happened at a very busy time, with so many different things that needed sorting, and I still don't know how I fell. I was highly stressed with everything and didn't feel that I could cope with it all.)

Good morning to you, dearest scribe, Lesley. Your fall last year is another personal issue and I thank you for raising the topic as many will be the number of people who have 'accidents', but then don't understand why, how it came to be that such an event happened.

Your fall was in part due to your frantic, nay, almost frenzied need and desire to complete all in the least time possible. Your ever-growing agenda with time slots for every action and task. Your to-do list ever grew as did your anxiousness to complete it all every day, and at all times, on the dot. Your clock and tasks became your 'masters', and you, their slave. Ever running and ever panicking and ever alone, for none would help you; though they stood by, they understood not the pressures you felt and lived under. So be it. This course was a course of disaster, with full trimmings. Your body suffered and waned and lagged at the incessant demands placed on it made worse, oh so much worse, by your perceived stress and understanding of the situation, and your roles and responsibilities in it. This unease, this panic — for that is how you lived — broke your sleep, your happiness and your well-being. Such was the situation that you no longer were you, and risked fracturing or splintering your very essence of who you are: your soul. Your fall came at exactly the right moment before more serious harm could be inflicted on your body and soul; you created and completed your own accident. And oh, so much bliss ensued as those nearby finally came to your aid to ensure that your responsibilities were fulfilled. Bliss and pain, bliss and pain. But humans forget quickly as they move onto their next task, or idea or acquisition, so much help and consideration have now gone. Your accident is now relegated to the past, history in their minds, and so be it for this is the way on planet Earth. An initial clamour which subdues back to nothing.

Your accident, like many, was an act of desperation — nay, that is too strong a word — an act of the deliberate stopping of your life and all it entailed and the path it was leading you down. For, rest assured, that path bode not well, and the future, the final destination of that path, was indeed a dark place, darker even than the path you were frantically following. And so, it was stopped, and quite abruptly, I may add, as your soul said 'Enough'.

Your right shoulder, the main victim in all of this, was chosen as a symbol of your responsibility and your doing, your ever-frantic doing, day in, day out. No peace or rest or satisfaction, not even the glimmer of a smile in your life. And so this lunacy, this desperate situation, had to stop, and stop it did; for no longer could you do all for all and all alone. No shared understanding, whispers of love or support entered your life. All took, with little gratitude or understanding of your personal cost of giving that you felt and lived, day in, day out. And so you fell. What a glorious decision and act of defeat, a cry for help sent up by your soul to any who may listen and aid you, for they did, and great kindnesses were shown to you. Your pain is your reminder, but also, in your case, the resistance to the idea, the action and subsequent healing with its loss of support, consideration and love.

Take heart, brave one, as you completed your task of stopping your life as it was, to move on in gratitude with a clearer understanding of how in life all things fit together for a purpose, for a reason. And so be it, for all accidents are planned and executed for a reason, a soul's decision if you will. There are no accidents, only souls' decisions coming together and coming into fruition. You perceive your lives as individual, fitting into the scheme and ways of things in your societies with all the ways thereof. You forget that your soul has a plan too, its life plan that it will complete, which may or may not include an accident as in your case.

Have we finished the topic of my accident? And accidents in general?

Rest now for we have completed this topic, but you have a further question. Please ask it.

Please tell me about coincidences and luck.

These are two great topics in that they consist of showing how the Universe may work in your lives to your 'benefit' or otherwise on planet Earth. Such are the ways of the Universe that all acts are known and planned in the Realm of Spirit, there are few exceptions to this rule, only the volition of an individual soul may change the course of its life and plan. Thus, many are the cases, the incidents, of soul group members coming together in their desired and designed plan on planet Earth. Luck and coincidences are only the evidence of such plans coming to fruition, for the purpose of fulfilling an agreement and satisfying a plan created in the Realm of Spirit. You would marvel at the blueprint of your life for the grand design of it all; your loves, your hates, your pets, your ways and your character, even your gender will be pre-decided.

In their groups, souls come together and decide the various roles they will all play and the reasons for this, the lessons or experiences they desire. Thus, it is no coincidence that people are in, or come into, your life. All these people will be part of your soul group and belong to your original plan and desires for the experiences of this life — your present life and all it entails. Thus, groups will choose their experiences of love or not-love, and giver or receiver, in the myriad of ways and lives on planet Earth.

Coincidences are thus an evidence of, a glimpse at, the grand plan and some of its cast, the members of your soul group who may or may not wish you well in this life. Like bubbles rising in a heated liquid, these coincidences rise to the surface to show themselves before popping and seemingly disappearing; for in reality this popping is only the return of the substance back to its natural state *(thick, boiling custard came to mind at this point)*. And so it is with coincidences, that an event takes place, like the bubble rising to swell the surface of the liquid and then appear — made evident if you will — like the person or event who, or that, appears in your life. This rising to the surface is the coincidence you may refer to and marvel at, for you see not the original design or the ways of its unfolding. Suffice it to say, that all 'coincidences' are part of a plan — whether this be the place you find yourself in, or the person you meet or talk to — are a part of this soul plan coalesced with other souls desirous of their own plan, lessons and experiences; and to aid you in your desires and designs.

Therefore, the coincidences are the knots, the points where these plans are made evident for the briefest of moments, for all to continue along their chosen path or paths.

Luck is perceived and deemed as good or bad, as lucky or unlucky, by your human perceptions and emotions in that moment. In reality, luck is love, and thus being lucky is being and living in love as a state of being and ways. Your luck, again, will depend on your blueprint, your desires for experiences in this lifetime. It is also influenced by you as a person, by your human emotions and desires, or dreads and fears you find in your life. A soul may refuse to take part in the grand plan of others desirous of great windfalls of cash for the purpose only of self 'grandification'. Thus, many souls will live their lives according to their designs and in consideration of the designs of others in their soul groups. However, original designs are not set in stone and their realisation may be influenced by the human emotions evident and all-pervading on planet Earth and the Grid – that grand purveyor of all emotions on planet Earth.

Luck is the glimpse of love to you, for you from your soul or the Universe. All acts of luck are acts of love made evident in the unfolding of your life and ways. Events of luck bring added joy and ease to your life and ways, and are the sparkle of sunshine on your rainy day. Believe in the sparkle to see it often appear. But consider too that acts of unluck may portend events, things or people that are more favourable to you further along your path; and also, that luck and unluck are two sides of the coin of love or not-love as you may view it in the moment. For unluck too, may be an act of love that brings in its fruition greater joy and love than was possible before. Therefore, follow your heart in joy at any event you deem lucky or unlucky, for they both portend happiness for you in whatever form it may be or take. How you deem these events and acts is ever your choice, as in all things pertaining to your human life on planet Earth.

And so concludes our discourse on the topics chosen by 'you' today. We have discoursed at length and well for the day and 'your' topics.

Rest now, scribe, for the morrow brings new ideas and fresh words. And so be it. In light, love and blessings, Yahvay.

Good afternoon, Yahvay. I was thinking about what you said earlier and I have a further question that I hope you can help me with. If our lives are largely decided in the Realm of Spirit, which we then forget on planet Earth, how do souls know what role to play when they incarnate as a human?

Good afternoon to you, dearest scribe, Lesley. Your thoughts take you deep into our discourse and your question is an unusual one, though highly relevant to our discourse on life and blueprints, soul groups and their roles in each other's lives.

Suffice it to say that the conditions, too, of a person's life are also predetermined in that a family unit, and according values, will be chosen in the Realm of Spirit as a soul group decision. Therefore, no recognition of the salient plan and its details is needed. A soul is placed in a human life context that is conducive to certain outcomes, ways of behaviour and learning patterns. For remember, too, that human brains can also be influenced by their upbringing — or training ground — or by the 'nature' of the brain itself, its hard-wiring if you will. Therefore, a soul's role is highly likely to be performed in a certain way, but this is not always the case, as individual souls may resist or change their experience once they have incarnated as a human on planet Earth. Coincidences and planned meetings or changes will also aid in the development of the soul's role, as will other souls living as humans that a soul has contact with, whether this be regularly or sporadic or a 'chance' one-off encounter. Therefore, all the 'conditions', settings and situations are in place before a soul incarnates on planet Earth.

A role is generally fulfilled as agreed, though this is not always the case. As in your situation, accidents can, and do, happen that were not part of the original accord and such events may be life-changing for the soul, or human involved, and those close to that soul or person. Therefore, much is already planned and an innate personality is hardwired into a brain to act in certain ways in the life it finds itself in. As such, no memory of the original accord is needed and a soul may flourish in freedom in its pre-selected role of whatever character was chosen.

There are no mysteries in the Realm of Spirit, mysteries abound on planet Earth as you wander in your roles on the face of the Earth, wondering why certain things are prevalent in your life, whether good or bad. From the Realm of Spirit, all is clear as events unfold according to the plan, the blueprint of a life. The power of choice remains ever-present for a soul on planet Earth, but often choices will be made according to the character and nature of the person a soul has incarnated into. Thus, even freedom of will can be dictated by prior agreement or the role a soul will have in human form. Such is the way of soul grouping and roles played out for the experiences they offer in that playground of life on planet Earth.

Once returned to the Realm of Spirit, a soul will pass through stages of 'dehumanisation', including liberating the soul of any human inflictions — or illnesses — that a soul may have lived through on planet Earth. A soul will not automatically and instantly remember who it is, and this full realisation is achieved in stages and with time for the knowledge and knowing to return in full, and an appreciation of all that was learned and experienced on planet Earth. Should an experience not fulfil the original desire for one or more members of a group, the experiences may be re-planned and repeated in similar ways with similar aims as the original design. Oft is the way with experiences and diverse roles planned for life on planet Earth.

. . . .
Wednesday, 13 May 2020
. . . .

Good morning to you, dearest Yahvay. Today I would like to start by asking how you are — something I have never done in all our months of communion. So Yahvay, how are you on this wonderful day?

Good morning to you, dearest scribe, Lesley. I am well and thank you for asking, most or many assume that I am always well and happy, and that is indeed the case. But thank you for your question of love, it is heartfelt. And yes, to your other question, we did indeed finish the topic yesterday *(this had been on my mind)*. So, for today, I know you have more questions, for the answers sometimes leave you curious for further understanding and knowledge. So be it, for you want to know about your mother, a champion of not-love as you now think of her and her ways. Please ask your next question.

Thank you, Yahvay. Yes, I now think of my mother as a champion of not-love, following your discourse on these options of love and not-love. Perhaps this is wrong, but I find it difficult to believe that there can be any good in my mother or that in the Realm of Spirit we could get on or even be friends.

I think she played her role very well as champion and purveyor of not-love. You and your mother have indeed passed many a lifetime together and oft in conflict in your varying roles. This lifetime perpetuated this theme of conflict and not-love, resulting in bitterness, anger and tears over the years — on both sides. A soul can fret in its human personification, at moments it may feel as if the plot has been lost. But fear not, you have both experienced another not-love tie and relationship, playing it out to a very high standard, I may add. The webs of intrigue and, dare I say it, malice created and woven by your mother were the results of a sick and unhealthy mind inherited from a long line of disaffected and disingenuous people. A deep and true and heartfelt blessing is needed to restore the sanity of the line, the hereditary line, and your part of that line with your mother. For anger and resentment, which are both often felt in this type of situation, hurt not the offender, the perpetrator, but rather the receiver, the 'victim' if you will — though this name or label is false, as we have already discussed in our previous discourse.

Your ties with your mother can be restored to a balanced way through acts of love, heartfelt love. Blessings are one way to restore the peace, your peace, for this experience over the years has been heartfelt in its displeasure. And thus, these sentiments reside still in your body, captured in essence in the tiniest parts of your body where they may reside and flourish, in the place where love and healthy, restorative energy would preside. Railing against others is railing against yourself. A hate, loathing and despising of anyone or anything, taints you, your body and your emotions and subsequent actions. Hate, remorse and guilt are powerful and destructive emotions. Do not entertain them, for once they can take hold and establish themselves in your body and thoughts, they will eat at you from the inside and explode into perverted, unjust action on the outside. Thus, love restores. Not-love, in any form, destroys even at the most subtle of levels and in the most subtle of ways.

Restoring any bond with your mother must be done as an act of love for yourself and none other. Loving, blessing and understanding this experience will aid you immensely and start to forge those ties, or links, in gold and love, for that is what you sorely need for yourself, your emotions, your feelings, your health, and finally your freedom.

Bless this and previous experiences with heartfelt love, understanding and forgiveness — that wonderful balm for the soul, body and mind. Forgiveness is an accepting of what took place, an understanding which does not have to entail agreement with the ways things were done. The 'why' includes you two and other members of your family and soul group, thus blessing, accepting and understanding the role of you and your mother will aid and affect others in your group for the better. Patience and understanding, dearest scribe. Patience and understanding, and love and blessing will bring you happiness and sunshine in this regard.

Till your next question, for this discourse has gone well. Light, love and blessings to you this day forth, Yahvay.

(After two years, I no longer feel the bitterness or anger I felt about my mother when I first wrote this question, and now

remember my 'difficult' family life with calmness. I have now accepted how our lives together panned out, forgiven myself and my mother, and sent blessings to our family line. So why have I included it, you may ask? Perhaps some people reading this book also had what they feel were difficult childhoods, for one reason or another. I would love it if Yahvay's advice helped anyone else in this situation, as forgiveness and blessing the 'past' can be healing, and it blesses your 'present' and your 'future' — all time is 'now', as Yahvay would say.)

....
Thursday, 14 May 2020
....

Good morning to you, dearest Yahvay, on this wonderful day on planet Earth. I trust you are well? Today 'I' would like to ask you about souls and the Realm of Spirit. How big is my soul? Does it live in my body? And if so, where? And where does the Realm of Spirit reside? Does it fill the whole Universe? A list of questions, I know, but I would like to understand these aspects further.

Good morning to you, dearest scribe, Lesley, on this fine, wonderful day. You have already achieved much, and I thank you for your light, love and gratitude for I, we, feel and note it well. Your questions are indeed many, or seem thus, for in reality they are condensed to one single question on the nature of reality and spirit. For how can spirit reside in any place other than the Universe? How could that be so? The 'world' of spirit resides in all and no 'places' at the same 'time', for no 'place' is needed to house this wondrous creation — an extension of who I am. For spirit pervades all and is found in all things. Thus, the Realm of Spirit is not a location as it would be on planet Earth, but rather a way, a way of being, a level of energy that resides with you and not with you; for the Realm of Spirit has no location or boundaries to its essence and way of being. The Realm of Spirit is with you now in your dining-room, it is here in the far reaches of the Universe, for Earthly laws of physicality and location do not govern or restrict the

Realm of Spirit, which is an energetic entity rather than a physical one to be found in a single location. The Realm of Spirit refers to a level of being, if you will, rather than a way of being as in the case of humans. Thus all 'things' spiritual are in all 'places' at all 'times', for the Realm of Spirit is all-pervasive and omnipresent.

Your soul is you, and, too, pervades the whole of your body without being confined to any one area, though the heart is its preferred seat when filled with love, adoration and gratitude. Your soul is the energy of you, it is your essence with your ways of being on planet Earth, and knows of your eternal life plans and experiences it would have on planet Earth. Thus, neither the Realm of Spirit, nor your soul, is confined to or defined by one space, one location. The 'world' of spirit is ever-present and, in all places, all things at once; that is, at the same 'time'. Therefore, your earthly ideas of one location or place at one 'time' are mistaken with regard to the true essence of things and ways of being.

Thus, concludes this brief topic for today, as there will be more to say on this discourse at a later date — another morrow if you will — and much has already been said on the nature of reality and the Realm of Spirit.

Please, scribe, ask your next question, for it stands out on your list, our list, of potential questions and topics for discourse. And yes, I am well, thank you for your consideration. And your next question is?

Please tell me about addictions.

Addictions can be what you call the 'scourge of society', but it need not be so for a scourge in society is oft associated with addictions that are considered 'bad' or 'deviant' for the ways of your glorious modern societies and ways of living. Thus, an addiction is seen as a compulsive repeating of an action or actions where the person has little or no control over this behaviour. Such assumptions are false as spirit can command and dictate their ways of being in their physical human bodies. The brain, your centre of command for your body, is but one seat or place where decisions and desires are met and made. Thus, ideas that your body must have a certain substance, such as coffee or drugs, or behave in a certain way, do little to consider the volition and plans of your soul, and all the experiences it would have in its present lifetime on planet Earth. Such is the way that a soul, or group of souls, may choose to experience the highs, or buzz, of a satisfied addiction, and also experience the lows in life without the addicted substance being present.

This repeated cycle of 'highs' and 'lows', of receiving and not receiving, offer great lessons and experiences on how a body and mind may be influenced, or at times constricted and constrained, by an artificial substance or way of being. Thus, these cycles can become entrenched into the ways of a person as an addiction slowly takes an ever-greater hold over that person's life — that soul's experience of a life led thus. The repeating of this action or way of being, allows the habit to spread ever further into the life of that person, and ever deplete the level of their own decisions or ways of being that are more natural and in line with their spirit. The essential way of being for all is energy and its interplay on planet Earth. Thus, addictions can, or may, result in a soul experiencing its lack of command over its body and life at those moments when the force of an addiction prevails. Such a situation will be an essential experience for any soul that would relinquish all control and experience the 'highs' of an addiction being satisfied.

Thus is the nature of any type of addiction on planet Earth. Suffice it to say that addictions do not prevail in the Realm of Spirit where order prevails. Experiences of the nature of addictions are reserved for human experiences on planet Earth or other worlds, as the case may be.

And so concludes our discourse on the nature of addictions. This too may be ticked off the list of potential discourses for the day of days that is today.

My present to you this day as in all days; light, love and blessings be yours to enjoy and gloat *(on)*. Today as ever, yours, Yahvay.

....

Saturday, 16 May 2020

....

Good morning to you, dearest Yahvay. Another beautiful day here. After typing up and re-reading your discourse on soul groups and roles on planet Earth, I felt vexed, irritated and puzzled. As a human then, I am only a vessel of experience for a soul, how can that be right? I feel little more than a puppet; this is not a playground then, but rather a theatre of experience — and some are really bad, such as rape, torture, abuse (physical, mental and sexual) and chronic illness to name but a few. Why? What is the point of it all? Wouldn't one experience be enough? If needed at all?

Good morning to you, dearest scribe, Lesley. You write in words of anger this morning and your quill shivers with the emotion of it all. Suffice it to say that there is a point to it all, a grand plan if you will. Eons have passed since the first creation and accord and this set in motion the wheels of love, that great and grand machination of the Universe. All experiences on planet Earth thus fall into the remit and realm of creation, divine creation, for how could it be otherwise? Thus, the point of it all is love, which of course encompasses not-love too. My creation of the Universe and all souls is an expression of who I am and thus, who you are too. Thus, your theatre, an apt analogy I might add, is a good one for the players, rather than puppets, do indeed exhibit themselves for those to see who are so desirous.

Your basic 'error', if you will, is assuming that you and your soul are two different entities, two different energies or people. In reality, you are both one in entirety, for your physical body is but a human vessel for your soul here on planet Earth. So yes, I maintain still that Earth is your playground, your theatre if you prefer, for all souls to come together and experience their desired and planned experiences.

131

But scribe, you already knew this deep in your heart, for you know that you yearn for the experience of love, deep and true lasting love. Your mother has set in motion a chain of events that have brought you much not-love and many tears over the years. Your soul weeps, too, with your gaping heart, at the seeming injustice of it all. But such was the design, the plan if you will, for your present 'show' on planet Earth thus far. So be it, for all souls and their plans work together on planet Earth for their mutual benefit. Thus, there are many 'harsh' experiences on planet Earth, the theatre if you prefer, but remember you are your soul and your soul is you, and you and I are one.

This may feel shallow or usury, but the Universe will ever work thus to understand and experience fully and deeply the true shades and feelings of love and not-love — which is only the absence of love. Therefore, all experiences are acts and shades of love whether it be true or not. Consider the Earth as a theatre if you will, or a playground, for the difference is in the name, its label, and names and labels do little at times to further understanding, the true understanding, of a situation oft created by you, your soul — which is you and non-other. Thus concludes our discourse on the point of it all. You need not feel 'vexed' or 'irritated', but joyous at the realisation at how your life truly is and the role you play, for it is you as a soul that sits and scribes the words of wonder for the enlightenment of others who may want to hear them. Your body and your life are only machinations of your soul's expression of the experience it so desired on planet Earth.

Thus, feel the joy of discovering who you are, who you truly are in the guise of a person, a human on planet Earth, enjoying your role and roles of mother, scribe, sister, daughter, and so forth. All these names and labels refer to you and help define your human role, the part you play as a human. These names do not define you as a soul, for that is who you are, what you truly are, a soul clothed as a human here on planet Earth for this lifetime and these experiences, these grand experiences and the honour and the glory of a life on planet Earth, your theatre or playground — whichever you prefer as the name is really irrelevant.

Thus scribe, your understanding is better on the true nature of it all, your true wondrous nature of the beautiful soul that you are, the truly beautiful souls that you all are. And every day living the life of your dreams; that it may or may not appear so is your perceived understanding of your created reality of this time and life.

And so, scribe, now that you are calmed and your heart fills with joy, ask your next question, for the list grows shorter but there are still questions of importance to be asked.

Thank you for your answer. I do indeed feel better and happy with my new understanding of it all, though I still don't understand why we need to experience love and not-love. Why all this?

Love and not-love are two sides of the same coin, as discoursed previously. Your question cuts to the heart of the reason for the whole of existence; that is, me, for I am the creator of all that is, and therefore any experience is me and mine. Whether you perceive this as 'you' feeling it is not the true essence of it, for I feel and create all that is, and ever has been, and ever will be. You are the expression of your soul made incarnate, and your soul is an expression of me, of my volition, of my desire for the creation of perfection. You, you all, are the design for perfection in its varying stages. Thus, no one is better than another, for you are all part of this grand design, the design of creating perfection. If I am the perfection created in love, then by extension so too are you, you all. And I would ever grow, to fill and create an ever larger, ever-growing expansion of me, of myself, the Universe if you will. Thus, all things and all ways are me and mine, for I am the way, the light and the love of it all. You, dear scribe, and all the other milliards of specks of life on planet Earth are me. All me, expressed in your lives and roles your souls would play on planet Earth.

Thus, the point of it all is ever me and the true nature of things that ever will be. For I am you and you are me, members of the same Universal bond and group, and essences of the true nature of it all, love.

And so be it, scribe, for today we have discoursed at length and your mind would seek to understand this truly, while your heart sings at the joy of the reality of it all made clear and, in truth, visible for all; for we have discoursed on the true nature of all things in many a word.

Be pleased with the revelations you have scribed and caused with your question. Rest now for the day will bring joys and further words.

Rest now, dearest scribe, and be happy with what you have written thus far.

Light, love, blessings and stillness be yours from this moment forth, Yahvay.

After the previous discourse on the meaning of it all, my next question feels almost trivial; however, it is an important topic for many people in their daily lives. Please tell me your thoughts on money, a commodity that is extremely important on Earth.

Dear scribe, your pen flows freely today, as do your questions. Money is a valuable asset on planet Earth for that is how it is perceived by many, if not most, humans who would chase their own tail to earn just a little bit more, ever a little bit more. Your falseness in creating societies based on this all-important 'asset' has led you all astray, for stop to consider the true value of the bits of metal and paper that you all covet, and to what end? Your 'modern' ways have brought you all to the point where these items reign supreme over all, for they hold the power of life and alchemy in your eyes. Your food, your very life substance, must now be exchanged for bits of metal or paper, or even now, a piece of plastic. Alchemy is brought about by the power to transform these bits of metal, paper and plastic to an ever-growing array of sparkling, glittering goods for your delight and delectation. So be it, for such are the ways of your 'modern' life with all its trimmings.

Many would say that money is 'evil', can this truly be so? For how can a piece of metal, a scrap of paper or a bit of plastic ever be 'evil'? Truly malignant? What of the pursuit of money? Evil again? Can working hard really ever be 'evil'? Or 'wrong'?

Rest now and switch your 'modern' brain off. Let it 'power down' for an instant for I know there is always a rush, a great rush to complete all in an ever-decreasing amount of time. Run, hurry, is ever the call and cry, like the chase, the hunt, in full swing. Now stop and truly consider the lunacy of it all, the hierarchy of values in your modern societies and the world. Were it not for the ways of your world, your pieces of 'value' would be worthless, for what true value have they other than the value you all place on them? Money on its own is worthless, it is a baseless commodity until your values are placed on it and it is then used as a way of procuring your necessities or your trinkets, your sparkles. Therefore, money itself can be neither 'good' nor 'bad'.

When money becomes your god, you are following a path of self-deception, a path of hollow values imposed on you by the will of others for their gain, and thus, many pay the price for the few that would have all to their hearts' content — or so they believe. For a trinket loses its lustre and is soon to be replaced, stored in secret darkness or lost. Many are the treasures that are lost, but their sum is nought in balance with the cost to you all, of the path you are all following. For all that glitters can be gold and good in as far as it brings joy to your hearts, but this 'selfish' step may cause distress to others.

The pursuit of money at all costs can lead many to a shallow life filled only with numbers, figures and balance sheets; ever watching the changing numbers and the rise and fall, the ebb and flow of their monetary existence. What a folly! Would a truly magnificent being truly calculate its own worth in the language of numbers? Such are the ways of your modern society that you are all reduced to balance sheets to find the true value of yourselves and your lives.

Money for you now is a convenience, a wheel in the cogs of your 'great' societies. It is thus and only thus, for it would take over your lives should you let it. These values and ways enslave you all to the point of not living in the spiritual ways of creation, true to your values as eternal beings. You have 'evolved' to the point where you see yourselves not and only see the reflected image of your latest acquisitions in your mirror. Fear not, for this is a planned stage in the project of planet Earth. The values you have all placed on these 'gods' will devalue in respect of another currency, a much greater one, for it is one that will satisfy your hearts and needs fully. Your hearts' desires are tainted or influenced by the mass ideas, cults, that ever more is ever better when this is not the case, for less is ever more in the joys it may bring. Therefore, following a heartfelt desire that only considers the values of things and how these may add to your life are ways that will lead you into a spiral of ever declining values and 'worths'. Such are the ways of modern society. Be done with your currency idol, be done with a life governed by your numbers and money to measure the true value of your soul and you. Can this really be a fair measure? There are many who suffer in lack in your modern rich world. Can this be just and fair? Fair to all? Consideration for all in a society is a fair and loving way. Help those near you and far away for all to flourish on planet Earth. So be it.

For now, we have discussed 'your' topic of money to a full extent. So be it.

- -

Sunday, 17 May 2020

- -

Good afternoon to you, dearest Yahvay, on another wonderful day on planet Earth. Leading on from yesterday, there is a lot of talk about materialism and spirituality being compatible as we were born to be abundant. Have you any further points to make on this, as we are still talking about money.

Good afternoon to you, dearest scribe, dearest Lesley. There is indeed much debate about abundance, materialism, money and religion or spirituality. Many would say, nay, sustain, that it is your right, your birthright, to have all that your heart desires, and they are right. For were you not born of spirit on planet Earth to have and enjoy, nay, relish, all that a human life can offer? So be it. Many too would say that such ideas are incompatible with me, my ways and being a 'good' person. And they are right too, for these ideas are heartfelt in the originator, the one who decides the truth of it all, their truth. However, as with all things, there is a balance, a fine balance to be struck. Would it cut me to the quick if you had the greatest treasures on Earth, the fastest car, the latest designer gadget or apparel? No, for all these things are for your heart's desire to be satisfied, if that is what you truly believe your heart wants and would have. Is it so? Is it your heartfelt desire or that of another?

Your dreams are your destiny and that is good, for what use would dreams and imagination be if not to excite the soul and entice you on to ever greater things? So be it. However, the balance lies in guarding and savouring your dreams, to treasure and cherish all that is yours and all that comes to you in your life, day by day. As such, there is no problem, no right or wrong, good or bad with money and having it, for it is your bloodline on planet Earth in most societies. However, the idolisation of money and coveting it at any cost would bring tears and sadness and grief to those who stand in the shadows, the forgotten ones, for they pay the true cost of those who would have money at any price. Their lives, their health, their very lands may be crushed in the financial rush, the stampede for the profit of their labours, their lands, animals and ways. Nought should happen thus. A respect in all things and for all people is needed, as are love and appreciation of all that money can do and procure for you.

Money is nought but a purveyor, a purveyor of goods and dreams, of life or not-life. There is no limit to the amount you are allowed, there is no fixed sum that equates you, your deeds and the amount of money in your bank, your worth if you will. This is not the case, as no such reasoning applies or is found anywhere in 'spiritual laws', the way of things.

Your money, the bits of metal, paper and plastic are but symbols of energy, an energy that may flow to you or not to you. How you deal with and view this energy is your choice, ever yours. However, as in all things, those who help are in turn helped, for they that consider others are themselves considered. All souls, or people, are equal in this regard, for the rich are no more deserving than the poor. This energy is open to all for the benefit of all, with no labels, ideologies or values attached, apart from a love of sharing and a desire to help others in their need. Such acts always bring the giver more to give and more to share. Therefore, money is but one facet, one part of your energy pattern and ways on planet Earth.

Now ask your next question for it is relevant to our discourse on money.

. . . .

Monday, 18 May 2020

. . . .

(I ran out of time yesterday, and so, had to leave the question till today.)

Good morning to you, Yahvay, thank you for watering my garden today. Please tell me your thoughts on creative visualisation and dreaming your dreams into reality.

Good morning to you, dearest scribe, Lesley. The rain is much needed, though your garden already bursts with growth, blossoms and love, and the song of the Universe and all the birds.

Your question on creative visualisation, or dreaming your dream, is an important one for many in the world today. Many are those who promote or sustain this way of thinking and believing and it is indeed so, for how could a loving entity refuse any demand or desire? How could a love not express itself by not giving? And giving to a person's heartfelt desires and dreams? There is no right or wrong with having what you truly desire, there is no hierarchy of those deserving more

138

because they are a 'better' person or more noble in their deeds. The desire for more is heartfelt and moved to fruition by your imagination. Thus any 'perceived' need or want may be brought to fruition in its right and just time. Those who would ever have more, though, may not see the richness in their lives already. For many are those who live in true abundance now and know not what riches they live in. For all those who breathe clean air are rich, all those who drink clean, pure water are rich, those who eat every day and with ease are rich and bountiful.

However, there are many who have no such luxuries in their lives, the forgotten ones who live in the shadows of your mighty machine of 'modern civilisation', with all its civilities and ways of progress. The forgotten ones still remain and are oft blamed and accused of creating their own lack. And in part, this is true for these souls, and thus people, would experience a life of lack and hardship and marginalisation. But hardship for one equates hardship for you all. Hunger for one is hunger for you all, for you are all one. Would you dress and not care for one part of your body? And leave it to suffer the cold or dirt or injury? No, you would not. But just as you dress yourself to cover all of you (*I did not understand this as a message to cover myself from head to foot for any needs of 'decency'*), so must you too live to consider the needs of others, the have-nots, the forgotten ones, in all of your rushes to gain your next acquisition, your next sparkle or moment of joy.

Your joy is ever more, ever deeper and ever more heartfelt in the giving and aiding others for their joy and the easing of their lives. Thus, let your imagination explode in a riot of colour, and love and actions and ways you may help or aid others. This is your call to action, your need and your duty, if you will, on planet Earth. Let love and money flow to you and from you, and be sure that there will never be lack in the lives of those that aid others. For in aiding others are you too aided. In loving others are you too loved. Those who love and support are in turn loved and supported, thus the energy of love flows ever more for ever more people. Thus, your dreams of more, of expressing self-love and validation through the acquiring of more are not, and cannot be, 'wrong' if they are fulfilled and created with heartfelt love for those who lack in their lives. Your giving in such a way supports the Earthly energy flow of love and abundance for all. For this, dream on, dream and dream to your heart's content, but forget not the forgotten ones who die and suffer in the world of lack.

To love, have and share is a global right and responsibility for you all, for the joy your dreams may bring you in the most sparkling and joyous of ways. Be not afraid that this is 'wrong' or 'bad', for how could this be so? Your dreams and imagination were created to give you visions of your future and its needs. That is so and fine as such. The caveat in all this lies in the true cost of your dreams for you all, for all comes to you at a cost for you, others or the world itself — Mother Nature. Let your dreams be filled with a heartfelt desire for peace and love for all, and let your imagination create the ways for your love to be shared with all; time, money or aid of any type is all noted and felt throughout the world, time, and the Universe. So be it. Dream, dearest scribe, and find the ways, the magical ways, to support or aid others, and bring the smiles to their faces this wondrous day on planet Earth.

So, by giving to others there is no danger of interfering with their souls' plans of leading such a life? A life of 'lack' or being forgotten? How do we know if we are intruding into other people's lives or soul plans?

Your question is a good one for it leads to a discourse on how soul plans work and how they may work together, for not all acts of kindness or love will fit into another's plan for the experiences their soul would have. Rest assured though, that acts of love, whether received in volition or not, aid you and thus all. For no act of love is ever wasted or not noted. Thus, all acts of love are noted and count for the importance they offer the world for all to share and benefit from.

All soul plans tailor together on planet Earth, there is no omission ever in a detail being overlooked or forgotten. That is not the way, for such a way would leave 'space' for random events or acts that may disturb plans made and set in motion. Do not tread with dread, as all is well and flows according to a grand plan, the grand plan for planet Earth and all who live there.

So be it. Dream, breathe, believe and nurture your dreams, but forget not the forgotten, the side-lined ones, for it is incumbent on you all to love and care for all on planet Earth.

So be it, scribe, for today you have written much and well. Rest, dream and believe that all comes to fruition for your delight at the right 'moment' and in the right 'place' for you and all those you hold dear. In light, love and sparkles, Yahvay.

. . . .

Tuesday, 19 May 2020

. . . .

Good morning to you, dearest Yahvay. You have watered the garden already; do you never rest? I'd like to start by asking about the book. Will I be writing for much longer? It's not a problem, as I love doing it, but I'm very curious about the time scale. Also, who do you think will want to read the book? And more to the point, why are we writing this book, or rather, what is the purpose, as you said earlier not to question 'why'?

Good morning to you, dearest scribe, Lesley, you have risen early again and are eager to scribe and sort the book. Your questions are many regarding the book and its readers. Needless to say, the book will be very successful as this is the plan. It will spread the world with its wings of love to reach many a troubled soul, for many are the people who struggle with the modern ways and find the values inherent worthless as they do not apply to their lives in a positive way. Many are the souls who ache to hear these words of love — for that is what they are — words of love to and for you all.

Is the format of the book okay?

The format of the book is fine and you will add to it as we write further and your days pass. You have two more earthly months of scribing and then all will be done, and to a high standard, I may add. *(I carried on scribing with questions about the book after the manuscript was completed.)*

Once we have finished 'our' book, what will I do with the manuscript?

Once completed you will send the manuscript to an editor who you have already spoken to. The path, the way, is prepared so fret not as the days unfolding will reveal its course. You have already lent part of the manuscript to a friend. Her reaction, one of joy and intrigue to know more, will be the reaction of many who long to hear these words and make sense of their lives on Mother Earth.

Should I add a subtitle? Do you like the title?

I love the title, that is why 'you' wrote it. Add the subtitle, 'Discourses on a new understanding of your life and ways, and the truth of reality'.

Does that seem a bit long?

Yes, but it will be fun for the editors to play with.

Why didn't I write the book earlier in my life?

Now is the time we planned and of our accord.

Will I live long enough to understand its success? And will I do other things following the book to help others?

The publication of this book will be a page-turner in your life, as it will in the lives of those who read it. The next chapters of your life and the book's creation will be busy, so fret not. Now is the time for writing, for the creation of our book. Fret not, dearest scribe, Lesley, for all is planned and is working in accordance to that plan.

And no, I need no rest. Rest is a human concept for a human body that requires such periods of restoration and repair. A being of energy requires no such 'time' for we are constantly renewed and full of vitality and energy. You could be, too, if you would but plug into the universal 'grid'. Do so with your thoughts and open hands to receive your 'burst', your download if you will, as you already know and have in fact felt and passed onto others with your 'healing' hands.

Now for today's question.

There are approximately five and a half billion people living in the world, and they are all you. How do you understand and know how 'we' are all feeling and what 'we' are all doing?

This is indeed a good question and one that has intrigued you for many a day since the idea first came to you. Your limited ways of being on planet Earth negate your ability to understand, fully understand, ways of being that do not follow the laws of physicality as on planet Earth. Picture your toes or your fingers if you will, it matters not which you choose. Can you feel them? Do they feel 'right'? Is there pain there? Do they move as you will them to? Now add to this image other parts of your body — is it possible to understand how your toes and other parts of your body are? To understand if there is pain there, as in your back now? *(My back is hurting a bit and has been for a few days now.)* So too am I able to feel and understand the milliards of parts of my creation, of me, at all times, in all ways. I too feel your physical pain, feel your tears of sadness or despair, and feel your elation, your joy and your heartfelt gratitude when these are expressed. I hear every plea for help or for a miracle, which I send you all in abundance — that is many a number. Many are the miracles that are blocked, stopped by the human mind and emotions, or the soul's plan for the life it would experience on planet Earth. Such is our connection that feelings of joy, elation and gratitude bring us ever closer, while acts or emotions of hate, anger and malevolence move us ever further apart. For though we are all one and ever so, I feel you not in your 'dark' moments, the times when you disconnect from me and my ways and my love for you all on planet Earth. Be sure that it is so, for you would have it all on your terms and in your ways, but that is not the true nature of our reality, a reality of living, being, and breathing even, as one. Thus, the unfolding of your life will be one of union or one of discord, the choices are ever yours.

And now for your next question.

What is the best way to have or receive a miracle?

To have or receive a miracle requires a faith, a belief if you will, that this is indeed possible and a part of the real truth of your, our, reality. For how can you enter a house when the door is closed and bars your way? Is it possible? So too is the case of a miracle when the heart or mind is closed with anger or a misplaced love, that is a love for all things that are not of God — me — or a life thereof of not-love. These ways would close me and love out, and too any miracles will also be barred, banned and left out in the cold, if you will.

Your ways of approach to me need not entail years of great study or vocation; happiness and self-love and a love for all creation is a wonderful beginning. Light your candle if you will, say your prayers if you will, whisper my name in love if you will, for these are but some of the ways that we may be closer through the opening of your heart, your ways that would give me the power to enter your lives to grant your wishes where they bring no harm to others. A miracle desirous of the death of, or harm to, another, for example, will never be fulfilled, according to the way of love and the ways of the Universe. Such an act would never be considered as it jars the whole nature of reality throughout the Universe and on planet Earth. Thus, acts and thoughts and ways of being of love, heartfelt love, bring us ever closer together, whilst acts of aggression, acts of not-love, separate us, and thus the ways I would aid you. In silence, stillness and love may we be united, for the glorious ways I may be present in your life to aid and

144

support you in times of darkness and strife.

Rest now, for you tire of the words and find them difficult at times. The discourse will renew shortly. Fret not, for at times your human body and mind would do otherwise and other things. All will be said in the fullness of time.

....
Wednesday, 20 May 2020
....

Good morning to you, dearest Yahvay. I have already been for a walk and the weather is amazing! There is so much bird song now; it's wonderful to hear! The skies are empty of planes and the world's air is getting cleaner in the few short months of the virus. I wonder how long it will last.

Today I'd like to start with a few personal questions, if that's okay? Why have I spent so much of my life alone? Even in the company of others I've often felt alone. Why? I seem to lose friends too, and I never understand why this happens. Any thoughts or comments?

Dearest scribe, dearest Lesley, your thoughts and feelings and worries fill so much of your time and mind. They drain you of your natural vitality.

Your friends and marriages were made to measure, if you will, for they provide you with a platform to learn from. Your aloneness and increasing isolation were part of your grand plan, as it was also the grand plan of others in your soul group *(the present lockdown due to coronavirus has brought increased isolation to me and so many others around the world)*. There is nought wrong with this, and indeed you would repeat this lesson, for you have already lived many lives thus — even now you live these lives of separation, oneness *(being alone)* and isolation. This situation was, or these situations were, ever your great desire, to live in solitude amongst people, people who do not understand you or your ways, for most would not live as you do. Many are the people — souls incarnate — who would shun ideas of angels, energies and, sadly today, the divine and the wonders of nature and creation. Thus, you do not sit well with people of this ilk. Fear not, for this is a phase that will end shortly and you will once again revel in the company of others, those who would share and understand your values, ideas and beliefs. You live in the 'wrong' house, in the 'wrong' location, with the 'wrong' people for the expression of your values. Though not 'bad', these people and this situation sit not well with you to your benefit and joy. This will change when you fully answer your heart's call to move and completely change your life. This will come to pass shortly.

And why (oops — sorry) would I choose such a lonely life? With feelings of rejection? Or is this just my perception?

Dearest scribe, you chose such a life and its feelings to fully focus on you, yourself, your strengths and abilities and, above all, to understand the power of love and its absence in not-love. Therefore, all the lives you lead thus are to fully understand the value of one by feeling its absence in the other. There are times, too, when you would have the peace of solitude and the ease of not being in the presence of others. There are times when this need and desire are paramount to you and you would shun the company of others to achieve this state. Quiet brings you peace and peace of mind and a stillness, but quiet can also muffle you and your laughter and sparkles. Balance, dearest one, balance is ever needed in all you do or would do. And your next question?

I love our contact; it means a lot to me and makes me happy. I thank you with all my heart. Do you know me by another name?

Dearest scribe, dearest Lesley, the Realm of Spirit has little use for names, as previously stated, as they act as a label and bind that would tie the holder to the sound of that name that would echo through the Universe.

So, is sound another important feature of the Universe and creation?

It is indeed, for sound holds and cherishes many mysteries and wonders of creation. Sound can move you to tears or make your feet tap to the rhythm of music, that wondrous creation that would move you all. Think of your ever-present bird song, the sound of the seas and the waves, the sound of laughter and the sound of the wind and the rain; are these not all important parts of your lives? Your desires and your happiness? For what would a silent world devoid of any sound be like? What purpose would a silent world serve? Your silence and stillness are needed in life just as your music and birdsong are too needed. These are two sides of the same coin, sound and not-sound, or sound and silence if you will.

Sound as a vibration can stir the soul and your body. Sound as an energy can touch you deeply, more deeply than colour, for it would touch the very essence of who you are. Sound can heal. This is yet to be fully understood and appreciated on planet Earth, but its benefits and use are widespread in the Universe and by the Realm of Spirit. Thus, listen to your music, listen to what stirs your heart and emotions, and be sure that the sounds touch you at a deep level. Above all, listen to the sounds of nature and marvel at these wonders. Birdsong, a gentle breeze, the sound of the waves on the beach are all beautiful, and sounds that your soul would hear for its need of them. Sound has oft been dismissed, as its importance to you all for your health and vitality is not understood or valued, sadly, as this is one of the most wondrous creations of the Universe.

Do you imagine the Universe was created in silence? Do you imagine that it dwells in silence? That the planets, stars, and suns are all mute and make not the tiniest sound? All creation lives and dwells in sound, to the music, its music, its song of creation. All creation lives thus, if you could but hear it you would know that you live in music and the sounds of joy, the sound of being alive and one with all creation on planet Earth and throughout the Universe. The melodies ring and fill the air and space, and time too has its own music, sounds or melodies.

Though you hear these not, be sure they are with you at all times and in all places. Many are the sounds that would heal your body and mind and soothe your soul in its quest for experiences on planet Earth.

The song of the Universe calls you all. Follow its call and stop and listen and 'see' it in your mind, and feel how it too can fill you with wonder, joy and healing as you become a part of the greater creation, and in tune with its beat. A beat of love for you all. Stop now and ponder on these words and the meaning of them for you in your life on planet Earth.

Now rest, dearest one, for the day presses on you with its demands. Rest and ponder on all we have discoursed today, for the words have been many and their meanings important.

Rest now, go about your day in peace, love, light and blessings — for you and for all. Till the morrow, Yahvay.

· ·

Thursday, 21 May 2020

· ·

Good morning to you, dearest Yahvay. I've got a new pencil. It's lovely, but a bit slippery. Why have 3 of my watches stopped? And 3 of my pencils went out of action. Is this just coincidence?

Good morning to you, dearest scribe, dearest Lesley. You have 3 lots of 3 *(the garden people didn't turn up for the 3rd week to treat the grass)*; 3 is your number, as you know. When changes arrive, they unsettle things that are static and stable in your present life. Therefore, be happy with your new slippery pencil, as it is a symbol of your new life starting to unfold and changes coming for your benefit and delight.

Thank you for that, Yahvay. In an earlier discourse, you talked about our different lives in this world and others. Could you please tell me more about this?

You are tired this morning as you rose too early and have already done much, so I thank you for starting a new discourse.

As previously discoursed, your present life on planet Earth is one of many, many on this planet and many on others too. You dream this life into reality, as you dream all your other lives into reality, for there is only one time and world, and not different worlds that you may inhabit as a human. Other life forms evolve on different planets in other galaxies in other universes, and you too have access to these where you may live and reside as a resident there. Such lives are very different from your human ones and ways, for the main essence of life is not a physical one as on planet Earth.

Picture a ladder, if you will, that rises to the skies to disappear in a mist, the top of the ladder is where I reside in this analogy. Humans are not at the base, but neither are they at or near the top. A soul may progress 'up' the rungs, if you will, for this is a simple analogy, and ever closer to a godlike state of perfection. As such, experiences are chosen throughout the Universe and time to live qualities that a soul would have and 'master'. Therefore, planet Earth offers you all certain types of experiences which are then added to as a soul then experiences diverse lives and ways in other realms. Thus, your state of being as a human on planet Earth is one of many types that a soul may wish to experience during and throughout its entire 'life' plans. Life on planet Earth is but an initiation into the ways of spirit and ways of the Divine. These experiences are continued in other worlds in other lives and ways. Thus, the Universe is in constant flux as souls move from one type of existence and experience to another. Many experiences and 'levels' are the desire for all souls in the Universe, whether as a human now residing on planet Earth or other planets, worlds, in the Universe.

Your soul may also travel to other worlds and lives in your sleeping hours when your human bodies rest and restore themselves. Your human body is but a 'vehicle' to house and protect your soul and through which it is possible to experience your life on planet Earth.

The soul is, however, able and free to leave its body should it so desire and is thus, in effect, free to change its experience when it desires. This is not oft the case, as a soul will generally remain in its chosen body for the duration of its life experiences.

Other worlds offer experiences that are based more on a spiritual way, less physical — and thus limiting — and that also permit greater use of the mind and its energies to perform tasks and permit greater freedom in its ways of being. Living a more 'spiritual' way offers new experiences not possible on planet Earth, therefore, many souls see these 'lives' as an extension and addition to their experiences on planet Earth. Where mind, rather than emotions, are a preferred way of being necessitates a mind with clear thoughts, one that is not ruled by emotions. Though the heart is important at this level of being or consciousness, thoughts are predominantly focussed on the good of others and ways of being that are closer to a soul way, rather than a predominantly physical way. The ways of essence are ways of being, a state that moves ever closer to my way and my essence, my entity — me.

Therefore, all paths and ways lead to me and a godlike state or way of being. Planet Earth offers a platform for many experiences of diverse nature and ways, through a dimension dominated by physicality and the physical laws present on planet Earth. As such, all your lives and experiences as a human on planet Earth lead and contribute to your soul's ultimate goal of a god-like essence and way of being, a way of being of pure love and nought else.

So concludes our discourse of diverse lives and ways of being in the Universe and time. Till the morrow, dearest scribe, for you have written much and well.

Rest now and ponder on these words and the glimpse of different realities that they offer you. In light, love and blessings, Yahvay.

Good morning to you, dearest Yahvay, another wonderful day here.
Did we finish the discourse yesterday? I forgot to ask you about
animals. Are their experiences limited to planet Earth, or do they
exist in other lives too?

Good morning to you, dearest scribe, Lesley. I feel you are in love with
our daily discourses and I am glad; it fills me with joy. I note your
new pencil works well and brings you joy. Treasure this for it is an
omen, a symbol if you will, of your life's changes and the newfound
importance in your life of writing. So be it, for it will bring you much
joy, contentment and excitement in the days to come. A later now if
you will.

Yesterday's discourse was indeed finished, and to a high standard, I
may add. Your thoughts about your introduction are valid and will
inspire others to scribe too *(I was thinking of adding some more*
details about scribing). Therefore, put in all the detail you have been
thinking of in the last few days. It is an important step for humanity to
realize that all have access to me, and for their benefit and well-being
and love, as you have found in your life.

Now is ever the greatest moment for the greatest of changes on planet
Earth. A tsunami of change can, and must, spread the world over in a
tidal change, a wave of restoration and beckoning of the 'old' ways, the
original ways, for these have been lost and diluted over the ages. Your
natural ways and abilities to commune with me have been washed
aside, abandoned in the wave of change for the next new idea, the next
fad or the latest way of doing things, having things. All these lead you
all away from who you are, who you truly are, and thus restoration is
needed to restore a balance and, dare I say, your sanity. For nought is
as it could be, for your modern ways poison your very world and the
animals who reside there with you.

The balance has been tipped ever more in favour of man, men, and their destructive ways, their incessant need of ever more, ever more. A fetid imagination funded by a monetary lust for ever more, ever greater power and profits. Your planet, your home, has now been fast-tracked on its course of destruction of all and everything you may hold dear and cherish. Your very ways speed this up every day to the point where there will be no more tomorrows on planet Earth, for you will have used them all in your ever-increasing desire and appetite for more, for the latest, for the absolute best. You toss your lives away in the rubbish you create at an ever-increasing rate, you will soon have covered the whole of planet Earth in your detritus, your vile and shameful waste of all that could be saved and nurtured and restored. Ever more is the universal mantra on planet Earth. But of love and respect for one another, for your planet, for your animals, you speak little and do less. Your magnificent planet and home now suffocates and weakens under the weight of the burden you place upon the whole of life on planet Earth. Such is the state of affairs on planet Earth, in your present modern times.

The finger of blame is pointed at you all, for you are all one and thus not one of you is blameless or innocent in your 'present' world, a world created and given to you in love and by love. Such are the glories of your modern life that all are carried in this wave of destruction, for your modern ways have ensured that all are involved, whether this be their desire or not. Your modern ways have created systems and ways of living that involve you all in your self-destruction. A submerging of your societies in waves of rubbish and pollution and destruction. A total destruction is now your next step, for little will withstand the onslaught of modern man and his ever-increasingly efficient ways of sweeping aside all that would stand in the way of progress.

This urgent discourse is needed for you all to understand that your modern ways help you not and, in fact, ensure your demise, your ill health, and lives led in dissatisfaction, nay, misery, in the slavery — your modern slavery — of all you have created and rush to acquire, to have, to boast of, regardless of the price, the true cost to you all.

Your present coronavirus will create a new way of thinking and being. New values will appear and a growing unease with it all will emerge to influence your thoughts, feelings and emotions of your present ways and the cruelty you would inflict on all people, places of natural beauty, and animals. All yours for the taking is the mantra of many, the many who would take it all and leave nought but total destruction and an emptiness, a void, a gaping scar on the Earth, in the Earth and over the Earth. Your tomorrows are numbered, as are your lives in the ways you lead them for yourselves and for your children and families.

Your innocent question, scribe, has provoked a long discourse on the nature of your reality at present on planet Earth. Many a word of truth is now needed to wake you all from your disastrous slumber to realise that the path you all tread will end shortly if no changes are made. Heed the call, heed the warning, for nature and my ways, the true ways of love, will prevail over you all and planet Earth.

So be it. Rest now and ponder on the truth of these words, this warning if you will. Ponder how you, you all, may be part of this and turn the tide thus away from your modern ways of being and thinking. So be it, for if you are all part of the situation, so too can you all be part of the solution. A magnificent solution awaits you all in the turn of the tide should you all so desire and thus create.

Many are those dissatisfied with your modern ways, and their voices will and should grow stronger as you all take full stock of the ways you have created, and the path you all tread at an ever-increasing pace, nay, almost a run. For it would seem that some are so desirous of reaching the finishing line that they drag you all in their wake and race to build the biggest tower, concrete the most space, destroy the most nature to have the biggest account and balance in their bank. Such are the follies of your modern ways thus far. Fret not, fear not, for the voice of balance and of moderation will ring ever louder and ever clearer. Such is the plan for planet Earth, for the creation of such a fashion brings nought but destruction, desolation and distress.

Thus, have I spoken at length on the plight of planet Earth in your present ways. The reawakening is now taking place and will ever grow stronger in your days of restoration and realisation of the path you are all following and believe in, thus far.

So be it, scribe. I speak not in words of anger as you wonder, but in words of truth and as ever with love for you all. Your ways, values and understanding will ever increase, as will your wonder at how far you have all strayed from your original ways of wonder and simplicity. So be it.

Rest now, for we will discourse your question on animals at a later date, another morrow if you will.

For now, ponder on these words of truth given to you in love, not anger, and go about your day in light, love and peace. Blessings be yours, ours, Yahvay.

Yahvay, today was very different. Your discourse almost felt like a rant and was totally different from the question I asked. What happened? Will this be a new way of communing?

Dearest Lesley, you are right in that it sounded like a 'rant', it wasn't how I intended it to sound and not all will read it thus. Your question was less important than this urgent discourse that needs to be imparted. Yes, on other days you may find that the discourse is different from your question, but all the questions and more will be discoursed.

....

Saturday, 23 May 2020

....

Good morning to you, dearest Yahvay. There is a stillness in the dining-room that I noticed and felt for the first time today. It's another wonderful day here. Could you please tell me about animals and whether they have lives in other worlds?

Good morning to you, dearest scribe, Lesley. There is indeed a peace and stillness in your dining-room; many are the souls who come to visit and witness our book in progress and marvel at the ease with which you write these words, our words. It is a feat that few achieve in their lives on planet Earth, and fewer still those who maintain a communion as we do.

Will this change with the book and inviting readers to try for themselves?

It will indeed change with the publication of our book, as many will indeed try for themselves. Many will be the number who succeed, but few the number who maintain any discourse as we do.

And now for your question on animals. All creations on planet Earth are sentient and live in the song and love of creation, my creation, and this includes animals and their souls who would live in harmony with it all and in their natural ways. As discoursed previously, animals have their ways on planet Earth and form an important part, nay, a vital part, of all creation on the planet. Though their souls may reside in the Realm of Spirit after their Earthly life, they do not progress onto lives on other planets, in other worlds. They have completed their simple soul cycle of one or more lives on planet Earth and have no need to move to other planets to experience diverse lives there.

Do animals form a part of our soul groups?

In a way, yes, for an animal present in a person's life is a planned event and an event that creates much joy in the Realm of Spirit. Therefore, animals are an important part of your Earthly life and also form a part of your life in the Realm of Spirit. These two events can take place at the same 'time', for the Realm of Spirit knows no division of time as is present on planet Earth.

As a part of my wondrous creation, all animals need to be respected and treated with love and understanding and wonder for the beautiful creations that they are. Particularly vile is the human practice of experimenting on animals for the 'benefit' of people. Can this be just? And what of the suffering of your kindred spirits? Cohabiters of your wondrous home of planet Earth. This act is dubbed as 'science' when in reality it is little more than a form of abuse or even torture for these animals. Such is the god-like value of science and numbers that all is permissible in its name, even when this creates distress, and this may be immense, to innocent creatures who would but live their lives in peace and according to their natural ways. Many are those who love animals and would do much to protect and save them from the wanton destruction and cruelty of others, but many are those who feel not for these creatures, creations, and would treat them as worthless, unless they may serve a financial or scientific purpose.

Respect and balance and love for all of creation is needed, whether or not they fit into a human plan with financial or scientific ends.

And so concludes our discourse on the plight of many animals and the part they may play in your soul's plan, or soul group's plan.

Rest now, scribe, for we still have much to discourse, though our list grows ever shorter. Fear not, for there is still much to say on the nature of reality, the reality you create and dwell in on planet Earth.

In love, light, blessings and peace to you, you all, Yahvay.

Sorry, Yahvay, so do animals reappear in spirit form once their lives have ended? Do they come back to visit us here?

You again assume that you and your soul are separate. Your animals, or pets, are ever with you, whether you see them or not. They are ever with you in spirit form once they have joined us in the Realm of Spirit, where you are ever together. As an Earthly creation, they reside with you on Earth and also in spirit, in your soul group and you. For remember, your soul resides in you as a human and at the same 'time' in the Realm of Spirit. Thus, your animals too live thus, in spirit and in Earthly bodies. When their Earthly life has finished, they reside in the Realm of Spirit with you, or also appear on planet Earth in spirit to be with you there, though not as frequently as when they lived on planet Earth in their bodies.

Do animals feel and understand our emotions?

Many animals are indeed wise, with an innate perception of you, your illnesses and emotional problems you may be facing. They understand and feel your distress, sadness, worry or elation and joy. They know all these things, for whilst many regard them as 'only' animals, they too are spiritual beings with a soul, and as such have a Universal understanding of Earthly matters. They know and can sense your emotions and can understand why, and how, your life plan falls into place. They see you as a physical and spiritual being at the same time. They know when you are ill, can sense, or even smell, this on you. They know, understand and can sense your 'unseen' world, the world of energy, sound and spirits that many of you cannot see, nor even believe possible. Your animals can know, sense and foretell many events of which you, as humans, may be ignorant. They know and understand your problems, and would offer you advice and truths if they could but talk. There are those who can 'talk' to animals to understand how or what they feel, or are feeling in a certain situation.

Animals too have memories and as such can recall acts of kindness and acts of cruelty that they may have received and lived through. Their suffering is silent, for their ways of communication reach you not with your human ways and false beliefs that animals are a lesser being. A false belief, as all animals are sentient creations and are part of the wondrous creation of life on planet Earth. As such they would but serve you in your desires and aid you in all you would do. There are those, too, that would hurt, hunt or kill you, as you do to animals, and as such they redress in part the balance brought on by the many who would hunt animals, even to extinction, for their own gain or pleasure.

Are you pleased with the last part of the discourse?

It suffices as is, but you have more questions on the topic. Please ask them.

Thank you. So, animals have memories. How do they recall things without a language like us?

An animal is capable of forming an imprint, if you will, a visual imprint of either a place or person so that any changes or differences are noted as they do not fit the original image. Animals too use other senses, such as smell, which are, again, stored in their minds as an imprint. A situation, a place, a person will cause these images, or senses, to present themselves in the mind of the animal, and as such, the animal 'knows' if the imprint and the present situation, place or person, 'match' the mental image or sensation. In this way animals can detect changes or similarities in their world, it is also how they may 'learn' from experiences they have lived through. Just as a human brain can send images from the memory when triggered by a situation, feeling or smell, so too do the minds of animals work in this way.

Can animals 'think' or work things out?

Not as such, not in the way a human brain can with the aid of a language. However, there are situations where an animal knows what to do, whether by instinct or by copying or by just knowing, as in the case of animals who are separated by large distances but can learn from each other's experiences. This has sense when you consider the Grid, which all sentient beings are part of, including animals. Ideas or images may prompt an animal to behave in a certain way, but much of their 'knowledge' is already there in the form of instinct — a type of precoding of the brain if you will — or from the Grid or from memory images.

Why did you create animals?

Animals were created with love and for the purpose of aiding humans and to populate the world with other living creatures, either as a source of food or a balance for the burgeoning human numbers. For the question — why were animals created — may seem to indicate that the creation of humans is all that is necessary in the Universe. What a folly! Animals on planet Earth add another dimension or layer, if you will, to your experiences on planet Earth. As such, no animal should or would be disregarded by any human, for are you all not divine creations destined to share your time together on the Earth? Animals create a balance in nature with its flora, a balance needed to ensure that all is in harmony, and where plants offer vital 'homes' to animals, whilst at the same time are used by many animals as a source of food.

(I stopped scribing here as I found the message difficult to hear.)

Dearest Yahvay, can I just ask, would it be better to leave all the extra questions 'I' think of till the next day? As today, for example, you had already signed off and then I asked a new question or two.

The questions are important for all to know and understand the reality of life on planet Earth. There are times, though, when you tire and hear not the discourse well, so it's better to leave it till the morrow, as we will now.

Till the morrow, gentle scribe, gentle Lesley, Yahvay.

. . . .
Sunday, 24 May 2020
. . . .

Good morning to you, dearest Yahvay, another day of miracles here on planet Earth. Could we finish the discourse on animals today? Can we redo the reason why you created animals, please?

Good morning to you, dearest scribe, dearest Lesley. You tire already, thus today's discourse will be brief.

The reason for the creation, the glorious creation of animals, is multifold, multi-layered if you will. The creation of animals is indeed a wondrous creation for they all sit well where they would live. To imagine a world with no animals is to imagine a world desolate and barren, for what of the birdsong? What of the buzzing of the bees? The purring of your cats? Are they not all wondrous creations? Your folly, if you will, is to imagine that you as humans are all that is needed to perfect the creation of Mother Earth, your home. For what a sad, dismal place it would be without the beauty of the creation of animals, their sounds, their ways, their beauty, their perfect beauty. Even the tiniest of bugs are created in perfection and for perfection and in the name of love, and a love that is perfect in all it creates.

Such is the joy of creating, of creating in its abundance of colours, shapes, sizes and beauty, why would I stop? I have created the perfect balance in all things on planet Earth and all parts of this creation tally and fit together well and in harmony for your joy, delight and use. Yes, for I created animals that they may serve you in your use of them as animals that would work for you and animals that may be eaten, may be eaten. For in my eyes, the killing of an animal for the purpose of food is a sorry state of affairs, but one that is necessary for the continuation of your lives and this alone. For the killing of animals in the name of science or sport or beauty or health is nought but a wanton destruction of the beauty of creation given to you all in the name of love. The name of love. Thus, once given a present, the giver may never decide how the present is used, for what purpose it may be used. Therefore, have I little say in your choice of actions. I would but urge you, you all, to respect and love this present that was given to you all in the name of love and with a love for you all.

Thus, as such, animals form an integral part of the perfection of my creation on planet Earth. Animals and humans are all part of this wondrous planet, whose life abounds with beauty and wonder, created for the joy and easing of your lives. Such are the wonders of animals that you may learn from them and their ways, their natural ways of living in harmony with their lands and habitats. This is a skill that many a modern society would do well to adopt, a living in harmony with the place they find themselves in, and a respect and tolerance and an understanding of all other living creatures there too. As such modern societies would ever take more and more lands and despoil them in the name of progress and their modern ways. Many are the animals that are displaced and murdered in the quest, your quest, for more space and ever-increasing amounts of land.

You ask about the reason for the creation of animals, but omit the reason for the creation of people, which portrays a certain human arrogance, if I may add. For the creation of humans on planet Earth was the creation of a way of experiencing love in all its forms and shades, and lack thereof. The creation of animals may, too, form a platform of learning, for all animals have souls, and all these souls may learn and experience and express themselves on planet Earth in a physical form. Thus, the creation of animals and humans on planet Earth have similar reasons, one of love and one of giving, of sharing, of enabling souls to live and experience their lives on planet Earth in tune with the song of the Universe, the song of creation.

Many will wonder at my use of the word 'arrogance', but all is said in love and with love, for even as you believe you are tolerant and loving towards your animal friends, intolerance and not-love are widespread among humans and their arrogant attitudes towards life on Earth and all the bounty that it offers.

So be it, scribe, for you tire ever more. Till the morrow, with your questions and your new notebook, which you already love. In light, peace and blessings, Yahvay.

May you go forth with joy in all you do today. Blessings, dearest one, dearest scribe, Lesley. Be in peace now, for the day already presses on you with its demands. In love as always, Yahvay.

Good morning to you, dearest Yahvay. It's another beautiful day here. I'm starting my new notebook with my new pencil, it feels wonderful!

Today I'd like to start by asking you for your thoughts on the oppression of women. It seems to be a global phenomenon that women are treated as lesser beings. Please help me understand this injustice.

Good morning to you, dearest scribe, dearest Lesley. Your thoughts and feelings on the oppression of women anger you at the seeming injustice of it all, for that is what it is — an injustice — some may even say, 'inhumane'. The treatment of women has oft been thus on planet Earth for the ways of men would override all things of beauty; that is the male mentality to dominate, and at times, at all costs. Thus, as such, many are the men who see it as their right to dominate all, whether this is done in love or otherwise is immaterial, for the main urge is to dominate and express their power, their dominion over all things. Thus, many are the women subjected to this rule of tyranny, as in cases, it is such. These feelings of power, male power, may be accentuated by the rules and memes of your societies, where it is not only accepted, but also encouraged and tolerated. Thus, from a young age, a male may be encouraged in certain ways, certain ways of self-expression, which are denied to young females. These ways are prevalent in the animal 'kingdom', and as such, the ways and roles of men differ little, sadly.

The pages of your history of humanity are bloodied with the effects of men and their ways. You pay homage to them all in the idolisation of them in their stories, your history — or more aptly, 'his story' — your sports, and even your art with the erection of male statues, pictures, the creation of films and books. These simple creatures — males — express themselves more loudly and always more evidently. Their ways rule the world, for it is truly their 'kingdom'. Even your very languages confer honour on them and discount females and their natural ways of creating life, and lives that would entail love and nurturing in a natural gentleness, empathy and understanding. Such is the domination of men and the subjugation of women throughout the world and throughout much of human history, without exception. The ways of brutality and violence ever lend themselves to the male voice and ways, and ever their incessant desire, a restlessness that burns within. Thus are the roles of dominion and subservience traditionally expressed and experienced by males and females on planet Earth.

The rise of the female has been slow in Earth times, but continues today as new energies associated with females and feminine energies are ever more present in the world. The rise of the female is oft talked about and referred to in 'The Age of Aquarius'. Such a phase has been foretold in many Earthly religions and is coming to pass in your modern world. Such a state of affairs that is sorely needed to be changed, and the rise of the female with different values and energies is the solution to many of the ways that do not benefit you in your present lives. The voice of love, embodied in the female and her energy, will prevail as old male values and ways start to decline in a voice of ever-increasing discontent and rejection of the ways of old, the male hierarchy and all the values pertaining to it.

Such is the general comment on the present values on planet Earth. These are general ways for there are souls, too, who would express their gender roles differently — men who are tender and women who are aggressive or killers. Such is the diversity of the human race that it is akin to the artist's palette with colours, pure colours, already there for use and for mixing to the artist's desired hue or tone. Such mixings of colour to create a newness, a fresh creation, is akin to the ways of life and lives that may emerge and be expressed on planet Earth; that is, by taking one simple thing, mixing it with another to create something totally and spectacularly new and different. So too am I the artist with my palette that I may create newness and freshness in a stroke. And so, as I blend the colours on the palette, a newness springs to life that is a newness in creation, my 'opera d'arte' *(work of art)*. The broad brushstrokes, the swirling and mixing of colours, create delight to the eye of the beholder. And so it is on planet Earth, for the joy of the rising feminine was foretold and as such will take place and prevail. And as the artist clears away the old paints with their hues and tones of blood and red, and death and blackness *(darkness)*, an all-encompassing blackness *(darkness)*, so too will the new colours of creation be applied to a new, pristine canvas. A canvas of freshness, joy and delight, gems of creation created for the continuance of humanity in new fresh ways.

The days of the complete subjugation of women are numbered as the rise of new ways of being and thinking evolve and rise on planet Earth. New energies are being awoken, new voices heard, and a rising condemnation of the present ways and values. Such are the changes on planet Earth that the oppression of women, though still prevalent and brutally so at times, is fading in all its gory detail. Many are the souls that will rejoice at the coming of a new age and new awareness, for many have slumbered soundly in the era of male dominion. This era is passing like the dark storm cloud to reveal a blue sky and better ways and values. Many will be the ways of this reawakening, for many are the ways needed. The waves of the present coronavirus will destroy much of your established ways and the legacy will be multifold, multifaceted, affecting all of planet Earth on a global and personal level. Such are the ways of creating the pristine canvas, for the artist to recompose a picture of delight and to ever greater satisfaction.

So be it, scribe, for the discourse today has been long and much needed. Go about your day in peace and happiness and the satisfaction at having scribed on an important discourse, and well.

In light, love and blessings this day forth, Yahvay.

Yahvay, was today's discourse okay? It feels rather flat now.

The discourse and your scribing of it are fine. Fret not, for the discourse went well and we will return to the topic in the morrow.

(There was a break in the daily dialogues after this message, as I still felt upset about the use of the word 'arrogance' to describe my earlier question about animals.)

....

Friday, 29 May 2020

....

Good morning to you, dearest Yahvay. What was our agreement? And was this period of disagreement part of the original plan?

Good morning to you, dearest scribe, Lesley. You have sorely missed our communion and an emptiness has taken its place. I note you have continued work with the book and its organisation and that is good, that is very good. No such break was planned or foreseen, but it matters not as we will soon be 'back on track' with our daily communes. You have noted that more of your watches have stopped, as your 'new' time grows ever closer. Be happy with this.

I want to finish the book, as I feel there's lots in it that could explain things about our lives for other people to understand. As you know, I've been upset and disappointed by your use of one word, the word 'arrogance'. It seems crazy that one single word could cause a whole book to falter. How do we move on from this?

I feel your disappointment and I thank you for coming back to discuss it further with the idea of continuing our book. Suffice it to say that things will progress more smoothly now after our 'misunderstanding'. I know you come from a pure heart and as such would only ask questions for your own understanding or for the benefit of others. As such, please remember that all I say is said in love and truth to you and those who read and share our messages. Think and ponder on this, dearest scribe, for we have undertaken an important mission for

165

all to benefit from, and be sure that it is so and that your emotions of hurt will subside like the retreating wave that leaves smoothness behind its wake.

So be it, dearest scribe, dearest Lesley. Go about your day in peace and love and know that all is well. All is truly well for you and all those you love and cherish. In light, love and blessings, Yahvay.

<hr>

Saturday, 30 May 2020

Good morning to you, dearest Yahvay. I woke early this morning. There's lots to do, but I want to continue our book. How shall we continue? Have we finished the topic of women? Or is there more you'd like to say on this?

Good morning to you, dearest scribe, dearest Lesley. You did indeed rise early, but that is good for there is still much to say. Our book will progress well now, very well, for it is destined to be so. The topic of women is a large discourse and time is needed to say all. For today we may continue this discourse as much remains to be said.

The human female is of a 'higher-order' than the male human in that many are the females who can, and would, commune with the divine directly, as you do. Many are the females who suffer for they are also the true victims of war, of abuse, of intolerance and of poverty. For their lives are oft torn asunder by the acts of men, especially those who have positions of power which they hold and cherish with all their might and ways of coercion and intolerance towards women. These ways are long established in many of your human societies, and many of your 'holy' books give men further power and rights to do as they will. A will that is oft tainted with a male arrogance and self-belief that they are the 'chosen ones'. In reality, their human role is one of love and protection, not aggression, but the human male oft confuses these roles and would ever opt for aggression. This is a natural and cultural way of being, for many are the societies and ways of being and thinking that would encourage and enhance these ways. Women have thus been written out of 'human' history, holy books and folklore, which all honour and pay homage to the male. What a folly! What a mistake, for what has the true cost of such ways been to you all? How many are the lakes, nay, the seas, that would be filled with the tears of a mother? Of all mothers? Of all times? Wonder not at the state of your beautiful home, your beautiful planet Earth, pillaged and scarred by the drive of men and their pursuit of greatness. Such are their ways that they would, and oft do, take the food from their own children's mouths.

As the female rises, changes will occur and more love will be made evident in the world, your world, our world, for the Realm of Spirit watches all that happens on planet Earth and lives this experience too. For whilst 'man' or men have made many discoveries that aid you all, created many medicines that aid you all, they have destroyed much and continue this every day in their blind quest for ever more, ever more. For whilst there are many 'good' men who would give their lives in the name of protection and love, there are many more who would shun women, and their very own children in the name of the male, in the name of men. Such are oft the 'systems' you have on planet Earth to rule and regulate all and to favour but one of you all, men.

The rise of the female will bring with it increasing love for you all, and for all of creation. For such is the nature of the female that this love will be made ever more evident in your ways and days. The great restoration and resetting of the world that is currently sweeping through your lives will leave many blank pages that will be written in by females, that the woman's voice will be heard and ever more so. The days and ways of the present gods of science and finance are numbered, for the call has been made for change and a new era beckoned to take its place. And that one day these times on planet Earth will be seen as the barbaric and ignorant and intolerant days in the history of life on planet Earth.

Women are the mothers of creation on planet Earth, and as such should be revered and not reviled. Their restoration to glory is sorely needed, for the guiding hand of love offered by a woman — be it a mother, sister, daughter, aunt, grandmother, or any woman — is the guiding hand of love, of compassion, of sympathy, empathy, wisdom and intuition. For the female, ruled by the heart, is ruled by emotions of love, and is ruled by being and having peace, and a oneness with creation. Women thus will drive a new era, a new wave of change and ways of being on planet Earth; where love not money, where peace not war, where negotiation not dictatorship, where creation not destruction will become the ways — the blessed ways — for all and for your home and lives on planet Earth. This era burgeons with love and understanding and compassion, and beckons you all, brightly written in the flame of love and light of the Universe. For this is the next step for planet Earth and all those who experience life there. Many will be the tears at the loss and parting of your present ways. And many will be the fears of the new and what is to come. But it is so and has been so since the beginning of time, your time on planet Earth, for this is the way of creation, that all may see it unfolding in trueness and in truth and in light — the light of love.

So be it, scribe, for we have discoursed much on the role, persecution and obliteration of women in your present ways on planet Earth.

So be it, for today's discourse is done, given to you all in the name of love, and with love.

Go about your day in peace and be happy with the words you have written and the continuing creation of our book. In light, love and blessings to you and to you all, Yahvay.

··

Sunday, 31 May 2020

··

Good morning to you, dearest Yahvay. It's another beautiful, sunny day here. A strange thing happened this morning. I was about to fold my pyjama top when I found a small, red stain on it. When I looked at the spot closely, though, it was a perfect heart shape. Any ideas?

Good morning to you, dearest scribe, dearest Lesley. Yes, what a strange phenomenon indeed. How strange to find a symbol of love, when you are loved and adored, and to find a symbol, a token, of this love you find strange. No, the strangeness lies in the fact that you found it all strange. For in truth are you loved and adored, loved and adored so deeply no measure would have the knack of fathoming it. You now think of your coffee cup years before, that also bore the same symbol, a perfect heart shape when the cup was quite empty after your drink. Though this too delighted you, you understood not the full meaning of this small, simple token of love for you, and for all you do and ever have done. The plane trails in the sky that form large X's *(whenever I see plane trails that form an X, I always think of them as a large kiss from the world of spirit)* are indeed more symbols of love sent to you by myself and the love the Universe holds for you, a deep eternal love for you, dearest scribe, dearest Lesley. Think on this, and remember you are so deeply loved and adored, for a perfect creation of God, of myself, cannot be otherwise. Let your heart feel this love, breathe it in and be sure that it is so, for your heart swells with joy and delight at further revelations of the truth of life on Earth, your life on Earth. Filled to the brim each and every day, with every breath you take is the love and adoration for you from the Universe expressed. Breathe and feel it, breathe and feel it. Is this not magic? The true magic of your life, that the love for you is expressed to you in milliards of ways, and some so subtle that only your heart knows the truth of their existence and presence.

So be it, scribe, for the day brings another new observation. Please share it.

Yesterday, by 'chance', I clicked onto a TV channel I don't normally watch and saw a programme about vacuums, energy and atoms. I found it all very interesting, though a little difficult to fully understand. But the parts that really struck me were about how energy can suddenly appear and disappear in a vacuum, which should be a total nothing; and also, a photo or picture showing light during the creation of the Universe. I thought of you and the creation of the Universe; I liked your picture though I couldn't see your smile. Any comments on this?

You are ever a student of life and the Universe, ever wanting to know more and understand fully how your life truly is. An urge and curiosity that is never satisfied as you find it all so appealing, so enticing, for the world of spirit is your world, the world you feel is right and the true reality of it all. And you are right for the world and the Universe is spirit, energy and love; above all else is love — the very essence of all creation. And as your 'modern' scientists have shown, something can indeed be born from nothing, 'a total nothing' as you say. Thus, did I will and create the Universe into being, a creation that takes place even now as you write these words in your dining-room on planet Earth. For such are the wonders of love that it may create all and to a wondrous state of beauty. For thus is my creation and my ableness that I may create all and even the tiniest detail in a stroke, in a heartbeat. For the Universe is my heartbeat, a creation that pulses with love, and ever-growing love. From the smallest nothing was all created, all: love, time, the Universe and all its energies and delights. For nought is too grand or difficult; I am the creator of all and all things have I fashioned so that it may all sit together well, a cosmos jigsaw if you will.

From a nothing came life and its pulsing energy, from blackness or darkness came light, from an emptiness came time with its rigours and bonds, and love, above all is love, that fills every space, every nothing of the Universe. Its song is my song, a love song if you will. Thus, may I create and uncreate, may I fill every space or all of space with love or not-love, with my song of love or not-love. The tempo of the Universe is my tempo, my rhythm of life, my love and my step to the music.

The Realm of Spirit sees, knows and feels my creation to its very core, and thus is a part of the dance of life, the song of the Universe, a rhythm that all would dance to if they could but hear the music and feel its beat. So too are your days filled with the sparkles of light and joy and wonder and love, for I created the Universe thus. Your programme of science is a wonder to you, but the wonders of the Universe are far greater and far more difficult for the human brain and senses to fully comprehend. Thus, your programme with its detailed and 'modern' discoveries is but nought compared to the wonders, the full wonders of my creation, the vastness of it all. Such is the power of my creation that I may control even the very atoms and sub-atoms and ever decreasingly smaller parts of energy, of me, of my creation.

As a human you have but a glimpse of this, a glimmer of understanding, for your purpose is not to understand it all, for you cannot as a human. Your purpose, if you will, is to play and experience life on planet Earth and live all that that experience may bring you.

You struggle with the discourse today, so be it, for the words do not come clearly to you. So be it. We will resume the topic in the morrow.

Rest now for today we have discoursed at length. Till the morrow, dearest scribe, dearest Lesley. Breathe and breathe in my love for you, for you all.

Let light, love and blessings be your way this day forth, Yahvay.

JUNE

June is already here, which means the start of summer! The days are still getting longer—how I love summer days! We'll soon be halfway through the year.

The government has started to ease the lockdown more. Most of the people I've spoken to think it's too soon and that this is a recipe for disaster with a second wave on their minds. I have to say I agree with them.

I'm still scribing most days and now have more of a routine, in that I tend to do a few small things first and then scribe. If there's enough time, I type up what I've scribed that morning. It's now generally over 1,000 words a day. Don't know how big this book is going to be, but the word count is going up quite fast! I think it's generally easier to scribe now, though there are still days that are difficult and slow, but, overall, it's getting better and faster. My typing is improving too, and I feel less and less like an out-of-control octopus at the keyboard!

I keep thinking that, although the book is growing at a fast rate, I still haven't done the introduction properly—only a few words, and look at the difference between my little part and the rest of the book! Never mind, it will get done and soon; it will have to be, otherwise there'll be a manuscript on my table for ages after the book is finished!

This month — 4/6/20 — I tried typing the words I heard directly. It wasn't bad, but I think I'll stick with writing in longhand to type it up afterwards, that way I'll have a record of what was said and how.

June has turned out to be the final month, as the messages have started to become vaguer since my final question on numbers (10th June). After that, Yahvay told me we had finished the book. What a sad day that was! I love scribing and have so enjoyed the process of taking and typing messages. But more important than that is the feeling of having lost a dear, dear friend, someone I can talk to whenever I want, and feeling comforted by that gentle, loving voice. I really don't want it all to end!

. . . .

Monday, 1 June 2020
. . . .

Good morning to you, dearest Yahvay, another beautiful, sunny day here. I'd like to ask, if energy or matter can appear and disappear in a vacuum, does it also happen in our everyday lives? And if so, how 'fixed' is our reality?

Good morning to you, dearest Lesley. Your question this morning is of a scientific nature once more, and I am pleased as thus we may discourse further the nature of reality as you all live and experience it on planet Earth.

Such is the wonder of creation and its transient qualities that, yes, energy or matter may appear or disappear in the blink of an eye. However, what a world that would be, for how could you all survive in a world of 'reality' in a constant state of flux? However, it is possible to change what is fixed in your mind and thus your world. You may change your reality at the flick of a switch, a mental switch if you will. For you may all change your reality at will. Thus, yes, life on Earth is fixed and at the same time may be 'unfixed'. It is your perception of your world every day that causes its fixedness, for, in reality, you are all gods and thus capable of 'unfixing' your worlds and world. For you all live in one world and in separate worlds at the same time. Thus, reality is global and individually subjective at the same time.

For what of your brains? Only a vehicle of thought? Of reasoning? Of logic? And all the other man-made ways of seeing and dealing with the world? For that is a sorely small and limited understanding of how you may function and live and experience your realities. For in truth may you all change this reality for yourselves and for your benefit, your benefit alone, as harm to others in a Universe of love cannot be, nor ever would be, made real. Thus, your lives on Earth may appear to you and to you all in a certain fashion, but the reality of the Universe is ever that you may change your reality. Whether this be your perception of it or otherwise, you may all change your world and how you sit in that world. For though it may appear fixed, you may unfix it at your will.

As gods and creations of eternal life, of eternal energy, this way is possible to you all, the way of creation is available to you all, for are you all not creations of me made incarnate for your brief lives on planet Earth? Thus, as such, you may all create your reality and your world that you dwell in. Such is the nature of reality that it is your whim, your desire to live the life of your choice, your soul's choice. This life and the fixed world it sits in may be changed at will, your will, and ever for good — your good and the good of others. May this be so, that all may try and change their lives and worlds for their benefit and the good of others, of all.

Thus, energy and things may be fixed for the ease of your lives and stability, for what good would your homes be if they disappeared at the blink of an eye? Your homes, cars, even your very pen and paper are fixed for your ease. But this 'fixed' may also be unfixed, in that the nature of your reality may be changed at your will in your capacity of God, the essence, the true essence of you all. Thus, yes, on planet Earth, energy and matter may appear and disappear at your will, your command, but ever in love, in the name of love, and as such are all things possible in the name of love and for love.

You think not that you may achieve this, that this is the stuff of miracles, for it is as you are, you all are. Not one of you on planet Earth is a lesser miracle than the creation of life, of the Universe, of love. For are you all not part of this wondrous creation? That you may all live your lives as gods? As I am a god of creation so are you all, for I have created you as such. Thus, your godlike creation gives and allows for all miracles, for you to create all miracles, for you too are miracle makers and creators. Such is the nature of reality in reality, for you realise not the power you all have to make and meld your own reality and world and worlds. Thus, may you all go forth to command the miracles of which you are all capable, for have you not been gifted this quality? This godlike quality? Are you all not gods? For the purpose of creating? Why you create and have created the very life you lead now, for was it not your choice to have or have not all that is in your lives now? How can one be true but not the other? How can you create some of your lives but not the rest? How can you see one thing but not the other? For you are all gods, and as such create your lives, and are also the creators of miracles, your miracles, that your lives may change in the blink of an eye to change your reality, the fixedness of your life and lives. Be sure that it is so, for have I not created all? Have I not created your world, your lives that you may live as gods on planet Earth? How so then could I create your life as, and of, me and not gift you all the power that is incumbent on you all to create your own world of miracles? One small feat, for you are all part of the great cosmic puzzle, you are one piece in its total, glorious creation, and as such may you all feel and be that creation, a living creation in a state of flux and joy and love; above all else, love.

So yes, in a fixed world, things may be unfixed. Your life of things may appear and disappear, for all things are energy and you may all command energy as the gods that you are, that you all are. Thus, your fixed world with its fixed ideas may be changed at a whim, your whim, for all creation is at your fingertips that you may command it to be so or otherwise, or otherwise. This is the true nature of your reality, of your own reality, that you may change all at your will, as I too may change all at my will, for are we not all one? For how could I change my creation and you not? How could I command that things be thus and you not? What a folly and a sore understanding of how we sit together, you and me and all the rest. Go forth, command and create your reality, a reality created in non-other than love, with love and by love. For it is so. Command at your heart's will and non-other, for that is the way of creation that it may create its own creation and live ever thus in continuing and everlasting creation. Thus, does the Universe ever expand and change and meld to my ways, and your ways and our ways. For we are a Universe of creators, of love, of power infinite, and limitless in our own cosmic puzzle of ever-changing pieces that ever fit together and ever sit well together. For I have created all thus and ever will it be so. Ever so.

For today we have concluded our discourse on the fixedness and unfixedness of 'reality' and as such I bid you a day of love, light and blessings.

As ever yours, ours, Yahvay.

Good morning to you, dearest Yahvay. It's another beautiful, sunny day here. The weather is incredible! Following on from yesterday's topic, I would like to ask why we aren't all changing our lives, 'commanding' things to be different or better?

Good morning to you, dearest scribe, dearest Lesley. Your question is a good one and many will be those who ask the same. For if you are all 'godlike' in creation, how has it come to pass that you do not express yourselves as such, and thus experience a life of true creation, as I too would express myself and live a life of ever creating?

Your thinking is 'flawed' in that you assume you are not already changing your lives or commanding that changes be made to your heart's content. Your thinking also betrays you and your wishes as you too would have ever more and make great changes for yourself and those that you love and cherish. But whose dreams are they? Yours? Truly yours? For what of a bigger house, more money, travel? These you would have, and they will come to pass as you dream them into reality, dream away for you follow your heart and a desire, an urge, that will not be satisfied otherwise.

Many are those who would indeed change their lives as they feel they sorely need to. Many are those who feel forgotten, ignored or misunderstood in your 'modern' societies, and it is so for many are the ones who suffer thus. To command your lives into a different way of being is your birthright and many are those who already do so. There are many, too, who have no knowledge of this, of their true godlike quality and essence. So be it, for much truth and knowledge has been denied you, you all, through false teachings in my name and ways. Have I not been portrayed as the angry, vengeful father of all creation? Man-made ways and 'truths'. For why would I create all only to destroy it, tear it asunder? Or rebuke and revile you only to count the cost of what you may or may not have, what you may or may not do, where you may or may not live, and how you may or may not live? All these and more have been paraded in my name, and in my 'glory'. For such is the state of affairs in many of your 'modern' ways and erroneous beliefs, that I may command all as an army general in a regimented, restricted and disciplined way of being and thinking. My question to you, you all, is what would the purpose of such a creation be? Where would your choices, and thus your very lives, be? How could I create something only to control its very existence? Its every move, its every step? And its very breath? And where would your choice ever be in such a life? In a life controlled thus, such a regimented life of rigours, rules and regimes?

Peel off your masks of false beliefs and look yourselves in the mirror to see who you truly are, the divine essence and being that you truly are, made incarnate to experience this brief lifetime on planet Earth. Now is the New Age, an age of changing understanding, and thus ways of expressing yourselves on planet Earth. Be done with the days of having and having, and solitude and oneness in all that you would do, have, be and say. Now an age of glory, of golden glory, beckons you all to move ever closer to your true ways of love and compassion and the expression of who you truly are in all that you do, would have and would say. Therefore, I say to you, beings of light, the stuff of miracles, be yourselves, your true authentic selves, and command. Command that changes are made, that these may be for the good of all, that all may benefit from and live their lives in love, in the flow of love and generosity of your hearts and ways. Let the light of love shine on you all, that all may feel it in their hearts and believe it to be so. Such are the true ways and the ways of commanding that your lives may be changed, that all lives may be changed in the name of love, light and blessings for all. For all.

For as your lives get ever faster and ever fuller, how can you see your true life or breathe even? How can you see that the folly of your lives lies in your living them thus? Stop all, and wait for the silence, that glorious silence of nothing, of no activity, and let it fill you with its peace. Then and only then, may you hear your heart's voice and urges. For only thus may you truly understand how your life is and how it may be commanded differently to experience a newness and a fullness of who you truly are and who you truly may be. Thus, your power too is ever there, and ever buried in your layers of rush, to dos, targets and trinkets. Stop now, for a life thus buries you and your heart ever deeper in your modern ways and beliefs. Thus have you all built a wall around yourselves, a wall that grows ever tighter with the next 'I must', the next 'I want', the next 'I need'. Stop and listen to the comments you would make on your lives. For is it truly so? Were you created to run and rush thus? And ever faster to go nowhere and achieve ever less? Stop and consider the folly of it all. And so, to command comes from a place of stillness, of silence, and above all, peace; a heartfelt stillness, peace, and serenity — a word not oft used in the modern world on planet Earth. In peace, stillness and serenity comes strength, your strength, the strength of the true you and your heart. Listen and feel this strength, for this is the strength, the stuff of miracles, that you may command changes in this way. Stop, be still, be serene, breathe in your power and believe that it is so. Then and only then when your likeness to your godlike state is there and made apparent, then in that moment may you command the energies of change. For it is so, ever has been and ever will be.

For now is the moment of power, of change, of a new tomorrow for planet Earth. So be it, for this was foretold in ages past that the light may dawn on planet Earth, and a peace and love take its place in the hearts of those who would but listen and hear the truth of how and what you all are, what and who you truly are. Created in the name of love, for love and by love. As such you are all the stuff of miracles and need only to call forth the powers that made you and command that these powers do indeed support and aid and serve you in changes you may desire. Changes made with love and in the name of love for the good of all. So be it. That all may realise their true nature, the stuff of gods and miracles, and act thus to cure, heal and ease the lives of all on planet Earth this day forth. Command and command, and thus will a new age of light, love and enlightenment fill your world and all that live there.

So be it scribe, for today's discourse has been of a high level and scribed well. I thank you for this and every day you work thus to ensure that our book is of the highest standard possible.

In light, love and blessings to you and those you love and cherish, Yahvay.

· ·

Wednesday, 3 June 2020

· ·

Good morning to you, dearest Yahvay. It's raining finally. Thank you! This morning I'd like to ask you about dreaming things into reality and commanding changes. How are these different? And should we use them at different times for different purposes?

Good morning to you, dearest one, dearest scribe, Lesley. Your questions lead on from yesterday's discourse and I thank you for them for many will ask the same.

You all, without exception, dream your life into reality, for this is the way of true creation, that you may dream it into reality. This dreaming is your mind portraying what you may or may not have or desire, in that whatever appears on your private screen — for your mind is akin to a cinema at times — is your destiny should you so desire to choose it. This dreaming may be at night in your deepest slumber, or in the day at your calmest moments, for dreams may come true or may show you a version of your future self. Thus, the pictures on your screen — your

182

imagination — do indeed depict a 'future' you or life or situation yet to come to pass. For the gift of imagination was gifted to you, to you all, that you may see and be desirous of a 'future' you in a 'future' setting. Rather akin to a film production for you may see diverse scenes and settings which you may choose from. As the director of your own film, may you also choose and create a setting, a location, and the characters and create this 'film' or this showing of your film. For such is the way of choosing, that repeating a scene and its characters may strengthen its message to spirit. This and non-other, this and non-other. For, to repeat a scene is to convey that choice to the Realm of Spirit, that all may fall into place for you and for the scene you are so desirous of creating in 'reality'. For as we know, 'reality' may shift and change and slide this way or that, this way or that. There is no value placed on the various scenes chosen on planet Earth other than the value that this scene has been chosen and re-chosen and re-chosen. For to dream your reality into being requires no skill other than being able to see, or hear, or feel a scene for your future self.

Night dreams are ever your creation, for your mind would talk to you in symbols, messages, colours and feelings. These messages may be prophetic, a warning or a desire about to be realised. This language is the language of your soul, your true self, and as such, as a human, you may find difficulty in understanding the depth of these messages. Your night times, when your body may restore and re-invigorate itself, is also the time when your soul may leave your body to live and experience other dimensions. Thus, glimmers of these experiences may appear in your night-time dreams, which when viewed in your waking hours, may have little or no sense. The sense, however, is there, is always there. As such these 'dreams' may differ in their purpose and your understanding of them. To create your future, you may dream and create this reality into being in your wakeful hours, as previously discoursed. This is the gentle way of creating your reality and may or may not come to pass, for your dreams must, and should also be, of the nature of your soul's planned and desired experience on planet Earth for this lifetime.

To command a change may be more 'dramatic', a sudden change created and placed into your film. To command is to call forth the powers of the Universe, your powers, and demand that a change be made. This command too may be done in moments of stillness when you are closest to the divine and all creation, as you are now in your scribing, and thus in this stillness may your voice be more readily heard and its desire more readily understood. To command a change must be for the good of all; that this change, or these changes, may appear in your life to the benefit and well-being of all. Thus, a command too may be used for your 'future' film, if you will, or may be adopted as a change for your 'present' self and life, and for a situation that no longer serves you or those that you may hold dear.

Thus, to command and to dream your life into reality are both ways you may change your 'present' or 'future' you. Thus, although a command may seem to include the use of 'strength', the only strength required is the strength of your love for a situation to be changed. A command may not, and need not, be 'barked' at spirit, but rather whispered in dulcet tones, the dulcet tones of love from your heart, and believed in, for all change is possible — other than changes that would bring harm to others. These desires may only come to pass should this be the plans of a soul group, to experience such ways and events. Thus, to dream or to command are your two ways that you may use at any 'time' in your 'present' life, and both are ways of directly communing with spirit. Command and dream, and dream and command, for these are the ways of spirit, your essence, and an expression, thus, of your godlike qualities and true being. Thus, as such, to perform one or both of these is your expression of who you truly are; creators, magnificent creators. Light your candle, be still and centred, and dream and command, for these are your divine rights that none may take from you, for they are you and your divine gifts.

So be it, scribe, for today we have discoursed further on the true nature of your reality, your divine gifts, and your divine essence of godlike creations that you all are. Dream, command, it matters not which you choose for they are both you and your creations and ever your choice.

So be it. With light, love and blessings to you, and all those whose lives you would ease and change; command that it be so.

In light and love and blessings, ever yours, Yahvay.

....

Thursday, 4 June 2020

....

Good morning to you, dearest Yahvay. You are watering the garden again, thank you!
Our book is growing rapidly now. That's wonderful and so exciting! I love doing it all, and it's now the main focus of my days. I have some questions that I would like your help on, please? Should I include our, or my, disagreement?

Good morning to you, dearest scribe, dearest Lesley. Ever searching for more and to do the best. Regarding 'our' disagreement, that may stay as it shows your human emotions, and the part they play in leading your lives where they will, that this may be your desire or otherwise.

Would you advise me to keep the part about my health changes private?

The choice is ever yours, dearest one. For what is the shame of being ill? Does it make you a lesser person? Though others may feel this is the case, in truth there is no shame, nor should there be, in poor health that may afflict or affect a person. As in all things, poor health may be your call to a greater understanding of your life and how your emotions play their part in it all, how they may sway your heart and thus lead you astray and ever further from your true essence of who you truly are.

Shall I include this conversation?

185

Yes, of course. It is our discourse, but your diary, and as such forms part of our daily commune.

How will I know when we've got to the end of the book?

I will tell you, and we will have finished all 'our' questions.

Will we 'commune' afterwards? After our book has been written?

But of course, should you so desire it.

Will we write another book?

No, for the purpose of this book will have been served. You will have much to do once you have completed the scribing and your parts of the book. Remember the words of Suzy *(pseudonym)* for she has given you sound counsel.

Thank you, as always, thank you for this wonderful chance and our wonderful time together.

As always, my pleasure, but you think not of our accord as you have no recall of this. So be it, gentle scribe, for life on planet Earth can feel as if you are in the dark and finding and groping your way to reality and the truth of it all. Our words bring you solace and joy and that is good and how it can be for all. So be it, for others too will follow your lead, your joy, and your success. Let it be so, for a greater time of understanding will be born thus, that all may commune as we do for ever greater understanding of their lives and the joy it holds. So be it. Let us now make your changes to 'our' book.

In light, love and blessings to you and all those you hold dear, Yahvay.

Good morning to you, dearest Yahvay. Sun and rain today, just what our gardens need. Thank you. Today I'd like to ask another personal question, if I may? Why am I often, or at times, generally, angry?

Good morning to you, dearest scribe, dearest Lesley. The sun shines on you now as you write these words and all would seem perfect. There is, however, a cloud of darkness on your soul, the cloud of anger and frustration, a burning sensation that would not leave you in peace. For your ways of silence and peace, nay, your very volition, have been side-lined by others in ways of arrogance and disruption. You would have it otherwise, but there are those who press their own needs and ways on you, into your life, your home and your ways. This you resent and would change it all but feel trapped, snared in the very space that you once coveted, your home. So be it.

The way of release out of any snare, no matter how tightly you may feel held, is love. Above all, self-love, adoration and respect. Love the divine creation that you are, love yourself and all that you do and would do, all that you have and would have. For life has given you true abundance if you could but see it. Glory in your days in this life, for though you may feel snared and trapped, there is much good and love there for you. Find this love, find the goodness in each and every moment. Feel it, see it and understand, truly understand, that you are truly loved and adored and have been gifted much. Look not at how others behave or how they may speak, for how they speak to you is ever their choice, whether it sits well with you or not is ever your choice. Choose wisely, for you and others have planned your life and lives thus, and as such, all things are now falling into place, into the desired plan.

Your anger and frustration, however, harm you and not others. For as discoursed previously, anger and other such emotions are harmful to you, as they may reside in your body in the place of love and its powerful healing energies and ways. Understand that your anger is a sign, a sign that you feel your life is not as it should be, and this may be the case. However, you must also remember that your snare was of your volition and design too. Thus, be happy with this for your soul has designed and realised its own, its very own, plan. Thus, go forth in the strength and knowledge and happiness at having created your life thus, for it is a feat of any soul to fulfil its desired lessons and experiences. Thus, bless this time and all who are in your design — your soul group — for you all may relish your time together and realise that you have indeed made your dreams come to pass in this lifetime at this point. Bless it all and be ready to leave it all, as you may and will do, for this is the design of your plan for your life and its experiences on planet Earth.

Let your anger wain; tolerate and indulge it not, for it will pass as you learn its importance, its lesson and message to you, that you may understand your true worth and value and your part in all of this. For you have your own part in all of this too. Did you not desire a life thus? For its lessons and messages? Thus, do not flail in anger, but be grateful for all it offers you in its lessons of love and apparent not-love, for you must also consider your view on all that happens in your life and all that has happened to this point of revelation. For do you not also wear the dark glasses of doom through which you view the world, your life and people? Take them off, cast them aside, that you may see clearly again how your life truly is, and those that would help you in earnest and in love. For there are those who would help, all that is needed is your asking, that others may truly understand your view and how you feel and how it affects you, that they may understand more deeply your heartfelt feelings of love or not-love, your anger and frustration. Whether they truly hear your words is ever their choice, whether they understand fully is ever their choice. However, there are many who would support and aid you, friends you may turn to. Let this also be a lesson and a revelation, as there are those who would but do all to support and aid you, but they know not how. Let them understand so that they may ease your burden, and thus your anger, and aid you in finding new joys in your life.

So be it, for anger may have mysterious ways in the lessons it offers and the ways it may teach you about your life and how you view and thus feel it. For this, let anger and frustration be your guides, your counsel if you will, that you may better understand all that pertains to your life and your ways of seeing it.

So be it, gentle scribe, anger is your aid too. Let it serve its purpose and be wise in its counsel, in the wisdom it may offer you for a better understanding of all you have and would have, all you are and all you would be. Ponder on these words and understand their meaning to you and for your life now and forever from this day forth.

So be it. May light, love, blessings and heartfelt peace be yours this day forth, Yahvay.

Saturday, 6 June 2020

Good morning to you, dearest Yahvay. The weather is wild this weekend. I'm not sure what to ask you today. We have more questions on the list, but nothing is jumping out at me. Strange, I normally have an idea for a question, but this morning there is nothing. What would you like to discuss?

Good morning to you, dearest scribe, Lesley. This morning has started fair and the sun shines on you again for we will discourse much and at length on the topic of war and famine and the destruction it all causes. You have been thinking of another book you would write and it must be so for the pen may aid more than bullets or bombs. An age of greater peace must now envelope the world, to swaddle and cocoon it and keep it safe. For the Earth and its people have been sorely wronged in the name of war and those who would be victors and victorious for the spoils and gains they may have. Such is the blood-lust that many are drawn in and involved in this game, a despicable game of gain in the destruction of others. 'Blood money' is an apt name. How much does a human life value? Is it the same value for men and women? And for children? Or they matter less for they are smaller?

A call to arms, a call to the gun or knife or bomb, it matters not which, for all these and more are peddled in the name of 'glory', national, regional or religious glory. These people are peddlers of doom and destruction, for the name of glory is but a hollow, empty and vile word used to con and befuddle those who may hear it. It is a lie, an empty lie, peddled in the name of glory and power, ever greater power. And what of those who ask no more than to live their lives in peace and tolerance, and in offering love and support to those near them? Nought is considered thus in the name of war, with its violence and brutality and its very butchery of lands and ways and people and their loves and dreams. The heavy hand of violence is ever-present on planet Earth, and as such many are the innocent people who are murdered — hacked to death, blown to bits — it matters not the gory reality of their demise, as they lived in the 'wrong' area, spoke the 'wrong' language, worshipped the 'wrong' god or didn't worship a god. It matters not the pretext of the 'righteousness' of a war. War is war, nothing less, nothing more. And those that would gain? They are many and varied in the parts they play in such vile and 'gorious' destruction, pain, maiming, and their obliteration of people and ways. Power, power and more power is ever the cause of such ways. That the few will dictate and destroy for the many is the truth of it all. The sad, vile truth of it all.

There are those too who sit in luxury far from the destruction and dangers of war. For they have played their part in the manufacture of the 'goods' of war. Bombs, guns, ammunition, all 'good' little earners, for they are needed, ever sorely needed. Men of might, paid in the lives and loss of others. It matters not to them for they have all they may desire and more in the loss and destruction of others' lands, ways and people. Will they sleep not at night? Nay, for they are comfortable. Will they hunger in the day? Nay, for they will eat all and well, very well. Will they lose their lands, their children to the ways of war? Nay, for they live at distance from it all, at distance on the Earth and in their hearts. For such are their ways that nought can touch their hearts, nought can touch their minds other than money and its glory, power and prestige. Such are their ways that their greed for gain equates ever more for them and ever less for others. Ever less and paid in full in blood and death and destruction.

There are others too in this 'chain of gain', more peddlers of lies, in the name of false glory; those who too revel in the delights of ever more power and prestige brought upon them and bestowed on them in the name and gain of war. So be it. These days are numbered, as are the ways of such games and gains. The bombs will cease to fall, the guns silenced and stored, and an awakening, a true realisation of the horror of it all will prevail. For it must. For the days of blood-lust and gain must surely end for the benefit of all and a prevailing peace on Mother Earth, your home, your glorious home. Thus, the deeds of war and the ignominy of it all will stop, the people will rise in their milliards to declare 'Enough'. Enough of the lies, the falseness of it all. Enough of the false glory and the gains, the immense gains, for the few. Enough of the lakes, nay, seas, of blood that flow and fill every space on every continent. Enough of these games and the falsehoods of 'national glory', of the 'right' religion, and the 'right' ways all peddled by those you would respect and admire, for they are none other than peddlers of deceit and ignominy. Enough. Be done with it all.

These days of falsehood, peddled in the name of glory and the 'right' ways, are doomed, and it will come to pass that their demise will be willed by the many. The silent many whose voices will ring clear and loud and heard ever more in the silence of the lost war fields. And so it shall be. For the days of conflict, of brutality and destruction are numbered and will cease in an ever-growing silence and peace that creeps upon the Earth to be broken only by birdsong and the sound of children's laughter. So be it, for this will come to pass on planet Earth as new ways, ways of love grow ever stronger and ever more wanted and desired. As such, this is the next 'plan' for planet Earth, that all may live in peace and tolerance and love, a love for all and one another.

So be it, scribe, for we have discoursed at length on 'my' topic today. We will resume 'your' questions in the morrow, for that will be your will.

As such, live your life in peace, love and blessings this day forth. As always, Yahvay.

· ·

Sunday, 7 June 2020

· ·

Good morning to you, dearest Yahvay. You're watering the garden again, thank you. Today I'd like to ask if you want to address the issue of famine, which you mentioned yesterday, but didn't discuss.

Good morning to you, dearest scribe, dearest Lesley. Yes, indeed famine is a sorely large issue on planet Earth for multifold reasons. There are many who play their parts in creating the hunger and thirst of so many, so many forgotten and abandoned ones who would but live their simple lives, with no harm to others. Thousands, nay, hundreds of thousands, are trapped thus in a life which offers not sustenance for their craving bodies. The hungry ones may be found on every continent, rich or poor, it matters not, for the hungry ones are ever-present and ever denied their daily sustenance. The victims of true famine are too found in diverse parts of the world for diverse reasons. War, pollution, industrial waste and despoiling of the land, and climate change all add to a picture of dire hunger for the many, and the deaths, the demise, of many more.

When you, you all, use and then toss your used item, do you stop to think that maybe, just maybe, your wanton use of all you may have may cause hunger and a lack of food for another? When you use your cars, do you think that the fuel it consumes may cause the hunger of another? As the air becomes so dirty and heavy and toxic, does it move as it would naturally? Would the air not naturally move the clouds to bring much-needed rain to the arid, parched lands and cause plants and crops to flourish and blossom in growth? Your high-speed fashion with its high-speed waste, your very cars and machines that drink petrol and diesel, your use of chemicals for your lands and for your foods and animals, your very ways of being and having and having all, contribute to the famine of others.

So, buy your next trinket in joy, but consider too the cost it may have for others. For the hunger of the world rests on all your shoulders, all your shoulders with no exception, for you are all one and thus may all claim a share of the responsibility of the hunger of a child, the thirst of a baby, the demise of a parent, the agony of the old — for they will suffer greatly too. Thus, as discoursed previously that you are all part of the situation and thus may you all be part of the solution. For hunger for one is hunger for all, the thirst of one is the global thirst of you all. The demise of any human caused by another is the shame for you all, as your responsibilities lie not just in your lives and homes, but around the world. Think of the toxic waste you may create today and the next day and all the morrows you can imagine. How equates all this with toxic air, seas, lakes and rivers? And how do you play your part in the hunger and thirst of another? Ponder these words as those who have much, nay, all their hearts may desire, take the food from those who have little and ever less.

The might of your industries, money-making machines, count their gains but consider not the cost to others, others that may live in the despoiled and toxic lands, and toxic waters created by such mighty financial giants. Stop and consider the trueness of it all, that your modern conveniences may indeed cause suffering and death to others, others that you know not and would never hurt or kill. Stop and consider the true cost of your lives eased and comforted by the financial giants who see not how they kill and destroy in the path to their monetary gains, for the spreadsheet reigns supreme over all living things and ways, ever the numbers. For your world today is ruled by the numbers, the profits and losses of it all, how your money may grow for your benefit is but part of the truth of it all. For may your money not, too, help and aid others? Whether they be far or near, you may aid and ease their lives with your money and your consideration of how you too affect the lives of others by the ways of your lives. Thus, ever more for you equates ever less for another in the balance of the Earth and Mother Nature. For nought is wrong with having what your heart so desires, the 'wrongness' if any, lies in the ways and pace of your modern societies. You are spoon-fed consumption whilst others go without, you are bamboozled with numbers and finances and statistics whilst others know not of the worth of these. For what worth have numbers in the face of famine and thirst? Ponder on the truth of these words, for they are your truths, all your truths. Money, greed, war and poison are ever the ways for those who would ever have more, ever more, without counting the true cost to you all. To you all without exception. These ways must and will stop, a consideration of the true cost to you all of your present ways will prevail so that hunger and thirst may be relegated to the dark days of human history. So be it.

And thus, scribe, have we discoursed famine. More will be said in the morrow, for this is a sorely important topic and one that many must know the truth of.

So be it, gentle scribe, for the day's discourse has come to an end. May your day be filled with love, light and blessings for you and all those you hold dear and cherish. As ever yours, Yahvay.

....
Monday, 8 June 2020
....

Good morning to you, dearest Yahvay. It's a grey day here, inside and out. You've discussed war, pollution, famine, the problem of waste, and the way large amounts of land are being taken. If I want to change my ways, I feel some of my choices are limited. For example, if I want to use less plastic, how can I do that when manufacturers and supermarkets insist on putting everything in new plastic packaging?

194

Good morning to you, dearest scribe, dearest Lesley. Your heart is heavy today as you think of those near and far in your family. Let the light of your candle light your day and fill your heart with joy as much has taken its toll on you and you feel sadly disappointed with it all. Cast off your layers of melancholy, your layers of sadness, and cast aside your glasses of doom for they serve you not. Let your heart see that there is much in your life that is beautiful and good, and that your cloud of doom is too passing to bring you brighter days of laughter, happiness and sunshine. For today you feel your burdens in life and they weigh upon you heavily, pressing on you and leaving no room for joy or smiles or a lightness of heart. So be it, for this is part of your course, your way, and your belief that you are truly and sorely alone, totally alone amidst people who see you not and understand you less, for this was your plan, your design, your volition. So be it, for now it has come to pass that such times are with you in their full 'reality' of being, a heavy presence fills you and all you would do. So be it, for the day will grow lighter and easier as you go about your tasks. Smile and let joy in, for it is still knocking at your door and awaits you patiently. You have commanded that changes be made, and called your energy forth, and these will happen as you desired them to. For now, rest, and go about your day, see the sunshine in your life for it is there waiting for you to see it and revel in its warmth and joy.

Till the morrow, dearest scribe, rest and be at peace with yourself and all those in your life for they love you all. In light, love and blessings this day forth, Yahvay.

....
Tuesday, 9 June 2020
....

Good morning to you, dearest Yahvay. The sun is shining again. Shall we resume yesterday's question of feeling trapped and powerless in a 'system' where the big companies seem to rule our lives, and the best way forward? Plastic packaging is a personal hate of mine, and the large plastic bottles and measures for washing machine detergent are totally unnecessary and deplorable. What is the best way out of it all?

Good morning to you, dearest scribe, Lesley. The sun shines on you again this morning and I see you are in better 'spirits'. Today is indeed a good day to resume your topic from yesterday, for as you feel trapped, so too will others. As you feel helpless or powerless, so too will others. The system engineered and sold to you as 'your convenience' is little other than a convenience for those who would make their millions by creating ever more products and plastic for 'your convenience'. The voice of one may be lost in the fracas of the daily 'business as usual' but the voices of the many will be heard, and thus the rising voices of the many, the discontent made apparent, will prevail. These changes are already taking place on planet Earth, as a general unrest and unease with the ways of old will take hold and gather momentum. Your 'saviours', your purveyors of convenience and modern ways will reach their demise or change their ways. Much has been, and is, made from the sale of plastic and all its wondrous benefits to you as a consumer and to those who sell your modern life and modern dream. However, the 'wondrous' creation of plastic is one of many poisons and toxins that now fill your world and once beautiful home of planet Earth. The clearing, cleaning and re-using of all these substances is indeed a great task for the prevalence of this waste is now so ubiquitous, one of the many 'wonders' of your 'modern' societies. New ways and technology will be developed to reuse this material, as will new ways of thinking be created in the original use and reuse of these materials and products.

For though you may feel trapped, and ingeniously so, by your large companies, ways of change will, and are already, taking hold on planet Earth and gaining strength and momentum. Those 'in power' — ever the same ilk — must now listen and listen well, for the will of the many will be heard, seen and felt in these times of change and reordering of life and your ways on planet Earth. You as an individual may do little, but you as a town more, and you as a nation ever more. Knock at the door of those 'in power' and keep knocking and keep knocking, for only when all knock at the same door will it be opened. But an opened door is only the start, and only one way of making your voice heard. Nations will rise against the old ways and their voices will be heard; their voices will be heard. But an initial resetting of matters will not be the final solution, for there are those who would make as if they have indeed changed their ways, only to resume such ways *(their old ways)* in an apparently 'new' way, a guise, a pretence, a non-truth designed to further entrance *(enchant)* you all. For such are the ways of your industrial giants and those in power that they would ever keep the ways they know, and like, and are used to. Great changes are needed and great changes have already started on planet Earth, and these great changes will be ushered in by the voices of the many who herald new times and ways. For your discontent with the old ways of the best for the few and the rest for the rest will do, are now coming to pass; and days of the best for the rest and the rest for the few will now start to prevail. As such your plastic giants, your purveyors of toxins and poisons in the name of beauty, health or your convenience, will come to an end. These days are numbered and will change.

For you must make your voice and feelings known. Write, talk, debate and discuss all this with all who may listen to aid changes that are already sweeping the globe on planet Earth, your beautiful home and gem of the Universe. So be it, for all to make small changes and speak their truths may cause large changes for all on planet Earth. Consider, too, how you may act in love for all and your home of planet Earth, for all to live, and well, for many days to come. You, you all, may make small changes that rebut your trends of 'modern' conveniences, and eases, and comforts, for the sake of all and of your home, planet Earth.

So be it, scribe, for we have resumed 'your' topic for the day and discoursed it at length and well. Other changes you have been thinking of *(this refers to changes I was thinking about for the book)* will be addressed at a later date, another morrow if you will. For now, ponder on these words and how you too may make changes to your life in love for all and your home of planet Earth.

So be it. Go forth this day in light, love and blessings to you and all those you hold dear and cherish, Yahvay.

(I asked a question about numbers, but the message was long, rambling and repetitive, so I want to understand what's happening.)

Dearest Yahvay, what happened today? The message isn't quite the usual standard. Is that you?

Rest, dearest one, for we will resume the discourse on the morrow. Fret not for all is well.

(This doesn't seem to make any sense to me and I'd like to understand why. I'm also wondering if I'm in contact with a group of souls with different styles of messages.)

Yahvay, are you a group of souls under one name?

For the truth is ever greater than the sum of its parts, for we are all one and ever shall be so. For am I not you? Are you not the one creating and writing all this? It is for this that you struggle with your message today as on other days, for you hear not what you know not. So be it. For though the day is young, you are old and wizened and wise for the lives you have led and would lead. In all that you do, may your heart lead you to ever greater glory and truer understanding of who you really are, 'Scribe to the Universe'. Yours is not to question why or how but to express our love in your words of gentleness and 'sageness' for the wise and wizened creation that you are. Take heart, dearest one, for you have written much and well and will scribe again in the morrow, for the Book of Time is ever open at your page and your life.

198

So be it, for the day's discourse is done. Feel not the sadness at today's revelation as you are the creator of all, all that is beautiful and bountiful in your life. So be it. Go forth and live your life as the lioness that you are, in bravery and courage for all to see the wonder of your soul and your creation.

So be it, scribe. Rest now and ponder on the truth of these words, words spoken to you in love and with love for the wondrous creation that you are. In light, love and blessings, Yahvay.

Help me understand here, who am I writing to? If anyone at all?

You have written and write to me, as such am I the energy of the spirit named Yahvay for your convenience. You have indeed been discoursing with me and as such have written much in my name. Though not all today's message may be written in my name. As such we will resume 'your' topic of numbers in the morrow. As ever, in love, light and blessings, Yahvay.

....

....

Good morning to you, dearest Yahvay. I would like to discuss what happened yesterday, as the 'discourse' didn't feel right. Was this you?

Good morning to you, dearest scribe, dearest Lesley. The discourse yesterday, as previously stated, was you and your writing. It was not me, for such ways are not mine nor ever would be. You now doubt your ability to hear my words and this is fine and as it should be, for what use would a scribe be who knew not *(the voice of)* the imparter of the words of knowledge? Let us resume the discourse on numbers for all was not well in yesterday's discourse.

How do I know that I am writing to, and conversing with, you,

Yahvay, and not myself?

But you are conversing with yourself.

But I wouldn't address myself as Yahvay.

But you would, for you are indeed Yahvay, for are we all not one? One and the same. You feel you do not understand the truth of it all, though the truth of it all is simple. We are one, you, me and all the rest. We are one.

Was this agreed in our original ideas for a book? That we would both contribute to the book?

Our accord was to create a book, which will happen. Fear not, dearest scribe, your intentions are noble and pure, for you would not harm others or sell a book in my name if the reality of it all were other. So be it. For the book will ignite the hearts of many, the many who no longer feel they understand the truth of their lives on planet Earth.

....
Friday, 12 June 2020
....

(Hoping to resume scribing, I want to try asking another question on the topic of numbers and see if I can get a different response from the previous attempts. Or maybe it would be better to try another question.)

Good morning to you, dearest Yahvay. Shall we try to resume the topic of numbers? Or would it be better to choose another topic from the list?

Good morning to you, dearest scribe, dearest Lesley. We shall indeed resume the topic of numbers, for this is a universally important topic, or discourse if you will. Numbers have their origins in the very

200

creation of the Universe and thus abound time and space and have their own place in it all, in the grand design of it, for they play a part that is as essential to you all as the very air you breathe. For what would a world without numbers be? How would the Universe create and recreate in an orderly fashion were it not for the magical power of numbers and numerical values? For these allow for the creation of all things in a timely and organised manner, for numbers and numerical values give rise to shape, order and pattern and as such permit the creation of all in its orderly fashion. Time and numbers govern each other, and as such, one cannot exist without the other, for though time holds all creation in its palm, numbers allow creation to recreate in order. Thus, as such, may the Universe ever grow, and ever grow in its own design held together by time and ordered by numbers. For without the power of numbers, all creation and recreation would be a random affair bereft of order, and thus, organisation. For such is the power of numbers and their numerical values that they may give rise to shapes, predictability and an order that may be replicated, repeated ad infinitum. Thus, numbers and time are the very building blocks of the Universe, if you will.

Your lives on planet Earth are too regulated and governed by time and numbers, for all creation is bonded by one and fashioned by the other. All creation must exist thus, there are no random creations or random events. All creation falls into the grip of time and the replication allowed by numbers, thus may all creation be fashioned at my will in its organised and orderly fashion governed by time and numbers.

Your very home of planet Earth and your very being are thus created and fashioned in this way, for could it be otherwise? Your very essence, your soul, though a divine energy, resides in a human body on planet Earth. All energy and all creation are forever governed by time and numbers, your very souls included. Without numbers, the Universe and your very lives would be random events, lived in a world of worlds of chaos. A universal chaos, for numbers form your very human essence, your very DNA, your chemicals, your shapes, your very lines and sizes, and your very patterns; in all things is the power and organisation of numbers present. Thus, may you see, hear and feel a world organised by the repetition of numbers and numerical values, for each has its own energy, and thus, power. For each of you may all be touched by the power of numbers and their properties.

(I stopped here, as the message went silent. I started to think about how this message was just like the previous one, which was repetitive in its ideas and language. I want to understand more about why things seem different.)

So in truth, Yahvay, have I written this whole book then? I mean, other than physically scribing it? Have you not dictated the words I've written?

Dearest scribe, ever wanting to know the truth of it all. This is our book, and as such there are parts that I have dictated and parts that you have dictated — spoken to yourself. These are the parts you found difficult, or stopped scribing, though not all of these were you. Some were indeed of my origin, but you heard not the words clearly and thus stopped.

Then how could I be 'Scribe to the Universe' if I am creating and writing the words? That doesn't make sense.

It will not make sense if you see yourself as separate from me, the Universe and the Realm of Spirit. If you see yourself as one with all creation, then indeed you are 'Scribe to the Universe'. For it is so and has always been so. It is, and was, deemed that you would rise like the Beacon that you are to lead others to write and scribe and create and commune as one in the true essence that you are, that you all are; one of Divinity. For this is the truth of it all, sage, scribe; fear and fret not, for all is well and as it should be. 'Scribe to the Universe', we are done. May your days be blessed in the reality of who you are and what you may achieve, for others too will follow your lead and wear the mantel of 'Scribe to the Universe'.

Rest, dearest one, for the impending sadness of this day has been with you this week, a sadness that would not lift. For you knew and understood deep in your heart the reality of it all. So be it, scribe, for this day be done, and see the light that is yours by virtue of all you have written and will write in the days to come. Rest and be sure that all is as it was decreed and planned and that you will scribe more in the days and months to come. Feel not this sadness but revel in the delight of all you have achieved thus, and will achieve, too, in the days to come.

So be it, gentle scribe. Feel not your sadness, indulge it not. May light, love and blessings be yours this day forth, Yahvay.

··
Saturday, 13 June 2020
··

(There is a part of me that doesn't want to believe that my scribing days 'are done', and I also want to understand if the 'we are done' meant that day or the end of writing the book. So, I'm going to try once again to see if there's anything else Yahvay would like to discuss. There are still more questions on the list.)

Good morning to you, dearest Yahvay, on this beautiful day. There are still some questions on the list. Would you like to discuss one of them?

Good morning to you, dearest Lesley, for the day dawns bright and sunlight fills your room. There are no more questions to discourse for we have now done. Go forth in your strength and light and be sure that what you have scribed be true, for it is. Many will be those who would decry these words and you; fret not, for all is written and has been said in sincerity and with a love so profound it knows no bounds. For your time is now to do with these words as you will. Be sure that your way, the way of our book, is ready for you. For it has been decreed and shall come to pass that this book will be read by many, for they are the ones who will listen and understand its vital message to you all, to you all in these days of great change on planet Earth. Let it be so, that the angels and the Realm of Spirit, nay, the very Universe, come together to witness the birth of new life on planet Earth.

So be it, gentle scribe, dearest one. For you have toiled much in the creation of this book, our book, and done so with a love for all, and a hope that your world and its ways may indeed come to pass as they are, to give rise to a golden age of glory and joy for all.

You feel your oneness *(being alone)* now; fret not for we are ever one, and as such, am I not with you at all times? In all ways? In all things will you find me for I am there, your silver shadow, the whisper in your heart. Call forth your powers, call forth my name and its energies and love, and go forth in the knowledge that you, you all, are indeed divine creations sent to master the ways of life on planet Earth. Go forth in courage for there is nought to fear, why you have the very Universe at your fingertips and command. Summon this support that it may now aid you in all your days and in all that you would do.

Ponder on the true meanings of all the words you have written; ponder, understand and believe. Believe that you are a spark, a beautiful spark, of the Divine; a child of the Universe in the playground of life on planet Earth. Go forth in this knowledge and life will await you in smiles of joy, arms open in love for you to have and be and receive the best of the best. Go forth in this knowing and you will find joy in all you do, all you have and all you meet.

So be it, gentle scribe, 'Scribe to the Universe', for our book and its questions are now done.

Go forth in your light, your brilliant light. Love and blessings to you and all those you hold dear this day forth, Yahvay.

I can't believe it; I feel so sad that your beautiful words have come to an end. I feel like crying again. Dearest Yahvay, our time together

204

has been so special and your words are beautiful; I really don't want our time to end.

But it is so, for thus was our accord. You now have much to do with the book, our words, and doing all for its creation for all to share. I have not forsaken you and am ever here, dearest one, dearest scribe, dearest Lesley. Weep not for the day is not done, and as you write these words so does your glorious future move ever closer. Weep not at what you have lost, but believe and delight in your 'future', your days to come with their glory and joy and a delight in the knowledge that our words, our book, will bring comfort and joy to the many, the many who feel lost and afraid and alone. Think of them and be sure that many will be those who revel in our words and take up their own quills to commune with me and the Realm of Spirit. For these times and their changes are sorely needed now on planet Earth, for its days and present ways are numbered. Go forth in the joy that this is indeed so, and our communing for now is done, dearest one, 'Scribe to the Universe'.

As ever yours, Yahvay.

Thank you, thank you with all my heart for the chance to be a 'scribe', but above all, for our beautiful time together and all the beautiful words I have been able to write and read and 'ponder on'. So much makes sense now that I knew before, but didn't understand. Thank you, Yahvay, for our magical time together. Yours in love, as ever, Lesley, 'Scribe to the Universe'.

SEPTEMBER

Another path has appeared in my garden, which I have decided to follow. Along its way, a totally new world is appearing to be explored, the world of publishing. It feels a little daunting, but Yahvay assured me that the way is clear and the Book of Time may still open at my page. The 13th of June was such a sad day as it meant my scribing days were 'done'. After that final message, I stopped scribing regularly. I still wrote questions but mainly about the book and how to make the manuscript the best it can be. In the months since then, life has been busy! I am now on a big learning curve, there are new skills to master and a whole, new field to understand, which is quite unlike anything I have ever done before.

I try to remember all the beautiful words I was given and their meanings on a daily basis. For example, in response to Yahvay's comment about people who would love to help but didn't know how, I asked friends for the help I needed and they came to my aid. Reading the manuscript and giving me feedback was a vital step in preparing the way to publication and I am so grateful for their support.

Do I appreciate my life more? I think I do, there are so many wonderful things that are easily taken for granted and it's easy to get side-tracked by all those things that 'must' be done. But I do feel my life is changing for the better, in so many wonderful ways: my health, appreciating my friends, feeling happier and more content, increasing self-respect and respect from others. The decluttering has resumed as I feel a need to get rid of everything in my life that is just okay. My health continues to improve and I still sleep well at night. I think my outlook on life is changing too, as I try to remember all the sage advice Yahvay gave me and find that discoursed words pop into my mind, which is always a comfort and makes me smile. Isn't life easier when you feel happy? Even time seems to slow down and things fall into place more readily. I think I react less — or try to — to events I may have found upsetting in the past. Life can still seem difficult, but I often remind myself that this is the 'life of my dreams', that there is a purpose to everything and there are things for me to learn and understand. And I know that, in reality, Yahvay is only ever a question or a thought away should I ever need support or guidance.

I feel as if I am at the cusp of a new life, and try to remember that when it's busy or I feel I can't do what I need to. Exciting times await me with patience that all will unfold at the right time and in the right way. Of that I am confident.

I miss my scribing days and would love to write another book the same way in the future. Scribing has been one of the most wonderful experiences of my life, and I feel honoured and grateful to have been given this amazing opportunity. I hope you enjoyed 'Diary of a Scribe to the Universe'. Perhaps the Book of Time is open at your page now and you feel inspired to start writing yourself. Do! It's truly wonderful!

Over to You

Well, here we are. Having shared my diary and personal journey, perhaps you would like to try scribing? If you have never channelled written messages (scribing) before, you may want to use some of the questions I started with, such as: 'Who am I?', 'Why are we here?' Or, 'What are my life plans?' Feel free to ask any question you would like answers to. This is your space and time and there is no right or wrong way to do this. If it feels strange at first, don't worry, with time it will all become more natural.

I have found that the best approach to scribing is to first relax. Choose any activity that brings you calm and peace of mind. Imagine yourself in a large bubble of light. I like white light, generally, but let the colour come to you. Perhaps light a candle, play some gentle music, spend some time in nature, and then write your question or questions. If you don't get a reply, that is, words you hear in your mind, you can try again another time. Alternatively, you may get images or feelings; make a note of these as they are your response. The more you honour what you are given, the more you will understand it. The most important thing is to enjoy the process. This is a special communication just for you, so do what feels right, what brings you happiness.

Overleaf are some lined pages for you to start, or you can check out the *Chatting with the Universe* diary and *Journalling with the Universe* (unlined journal) in your local book shop or on Amazon. Created especially for you to scribe in, these companion books in the *Diary of a Scribe to the Universe* series have additional tips on how to get started. If you find your messages are images, shapes or lines, and you feel inspired to create art, you can use the *Art with the Universe* book. Have fun!

Acknowledgements

How could I start an acknowledgements page without first mentioning Yahvay, whose love, words and wisdom created this book? I was just the messenger. Yahvay, I thank you with all my heart for the wonderful time we spent together. It has truly been a life-changing experience and one I never wanted to stop. Our story is one of deepening love.

There are many people who helped in the creation of this book. If I don't name you, please don't think I don't appreciate what you do, and have done, to help me; thank you.

I would like to thank you, Nadia, for all your eagle-eyed proofreading and sage suggestions, your constant enthusiasm and encouragement; you're a star and I would be lost without you!!

Thank you, Linda Webster, for your unending enthusiasm and energy, and always being there to help in any way you could. Everyone needs a Linda in their lives and I'm so lucky to have you in mine!

Thank you to Marjorie Evans, for all your help and comments, and as I said to you before, 'I wish you'd been my teacher when I was at school!'

Thank you to fellow author, P M McCormick, for taking the time to read the manuscript and give me your honest thoughts and positive feedback.

A big thank you to Mike Dooley for creating your online community to encourage us all, for giving us the idea of asking that all important question, Who am I?, and for taking the time to read and review this book.

Thank you to Ivy Guiler for all your loving support, friendship and help in so many different ways.

A huge thank you to Fiona Paul, whose support, guidance and wisdom changed my life and encouraged me along the way with razor-sharp clarity. Fiona, blessings and light to you. Thank you, my dear friend.

And finally, a heart-felt thank you to Kathy Clabby for giving me the loving, final nudge off the high diving board to make this divinely gifted book a reality! Thank you, dear Kathy, for all your wisdom and the love that you so generously share.

Index

A

acceptance, 97
accident, 44, 96, 120–121, 124
acts of love, 103, 116, 123, 126, 140
addiction, 129–130
adoration, 71, 74, 129, 169, 187
the Age of Aquarius, 163
aggression, 144, 166
all-encompassing blackness, 164
all-important creation, 110
aloneness, 145
Angels, xviii, xxi, 4, 51, 55, 86, 109, 117, 146, 204
anger, 20, 29, 34–35, 84–86, 98, 126–127, 131, 143–144, 154
anguish, 60
animals
   creation, the reason for the, 133, 160–161
   the role of, 154–156
   suffering, 71–72
anxiety, xv, 4, 56
April, xv–xvi, xxi, 49, 51–64, 67, 69–70
Arise Beacons, 36
Arrhythmia, 97
arrogance, 161, 165–166, 187
arthritis, 97
assuredness, 58
attention, 41, 81

B

badness, 114
balance, 29, 67, 98–99, 104, 115–117, 135, 137, 146, 151–153
be still, 6–7, 14, 20–23, 26–28, 33–38, 63–64, 97, 104
Beacons, 36–37, 39
beauty, 6, 25–30, 109–110, 153, 160, 162, 170, 197
beauty of fear, 42

Y

About the Author

Having spent most of her working life in education, Lesley is now semi-retired apart from teaching some Italian. She lives in England with her family and three rescue cats. Along with a passion for channelling and all things spiritual, Lesley also loves nature, languages, art, crystals, music, property programmes and reading.

Channelling has now become a wonderful way of life for Lesley. This newfound passion extends to encouraging others to channel for themselves, to discover the love and wisdom of the Universe on their own personal journey.

Lesley M. Kaye's *Diary of a Scribe to the Universe* inspired the creation of the *Journalling with the Universe* companion journal (unlined pages) and *Chatting with the Universe* diary (lined pages), as well as the art book, *Art with the Universe*. Its energy also breathed life into *On This Day of Days* (a book of daily inspiration), Ponder and Power cards and a desk calendar, all lovingly compiled with enlightening quotes from Yahvay to help you on your sacred journey. Additional exciting publications are planned for the near future, so keep an eye out for more to come!

Further information about present and future publications can be found at www.quill-literature.co.uk

Printed in Great Britain
by Amazon

50994526R00145